ARMAMENT AND TECHNOLOGY

TRANSPORT AIRCRAFT

— AND SPECIALIZED CARRIERS —

Illustrations: Octavio Díez Cámara, Construcciones Aeronáuticas S.A, Lockheed Martin, McDonnell Douglas Corporation, Dassault Aviation, British Aerospace, Daimler-Benz Aerospace, Ejército del Aire Español, United States Navy, Aermachi S.p.A., Northrop Grumman Corporation, Raytheon E-Systems, Hughes Aircraft, Eurocopter, Spetztekhnika, Kongsberg Gruppen ASA, Matra BAE Dynamics, François Robineau, Pere Redón Trabal and Antonio Ros Pau.

Production: Ediciones Lema, S.L.
Editorial Director: Josep M. Parramón Homs
Original text: Octavio Díez
Original title: 'Aviones de Transporte y Especializados'
Translation: Mike Roberts
Coordination. Victoria Sánchez and Eduardo Hernández

I.S.B.N. 84-95323-17-6

Photosetting and photomechanics: Novasis, S.A.L.
Barcelona (Spain)
Printed in Spain

TRANSPORT AIRCRAFT
AND SPECIALIZED CARRIERS

LEMA
Publications

n 1996, after two million hours of operation, the C-212 celebrated its 25th anniversary. More than 450 C-212s are now used by 84 operators in 40 countries. Over the years they have proven sturdy, reliable and easy to operate and maintain. The multipurpose design has led to this light transport plane being used for a wide variety of military and civilian tasks.

Origin

The C-212 originated from a decision made by the Spanish Air Force (Ejército del Aire – EA) to renovate its fleet with a home-produced product, that would meet the requirements of minimum cost and maximum efficiency. With these targets in mind, based on the ideas of earlier projects such as the C-208 and the C-211, a development team was formed in 1968. Led by the aeronautics technical engineer Juan

PATROL

Designed for patrol and maritime vigilance, the special version of "Aviocar" is used in, among other countries, Spain, Portugal and Argentina. It has been chosen for its multipurpose characteristics, large capacity and simple operation.

EXPORTED

The C-212 has been a huge sales success, with more than 450 models being used in military and civilian missions in 40 countries.

Antonio Mariano. A full-scale wooden model was constructed, and the EA participated in the final design of the cockpit.

The project became a reality with the building of two aircraft and the ground testing equipment at a factory in Getafe, near Madrid. The small group of workers was supported by Project Finance staff and the Spanish National Institute of Aerospace Technology (INTA).

Pre-production

Once ground testing had been completed, the first flight took place on the 26th March 1971, and led to the Spanish Air Ministry contracting six photographic

surveillance planes and two to be used for air training, to which the producers, Construcciones Aeronáuticas, SA (CASA) added two more for demonstration purposes.

The first pre-production plane flew on the 17th November 1972, after which the EA ordered 29 vehicles with capacity for two tons of general cargo or 16 parachutists, along with three training vehicles. The first foreign orders came in 1974 when the Portuguese Air Force requested 24 aeroplanes. Orders came later from Jordan and Indonesia, taking 1977 production up to three units a month, and later still from the military forces of Thailand, Venezuela, Uruguay, Abu-Dhabi, Panama, Mexico, Bolivia, Colombia, Chile, France, Lesotho, Sweden, Ireland and a long list of countries that used approximately half the total number of vehicles produced.

> **UPDATED**
> At a recent show in Le Bourget, CASA presented the 400 Series of "Aviocar" which incorporates several technological innovations, such as an advanced digital cockpit which meets the transport demands of the new century.

Extraction System– which meant installing an A/M-100 system in the landing bay. Frontier vigilance and ELINT (electronic intelligence) with special antennas and consoles for the three cockpit operators, calibration of radio assistance, the evacuation of medical equipment and stretchers and much more. Vehicles destined for the civilian market are equipped with rows of seats and are prepared for any kind of load or passengers that may be required.

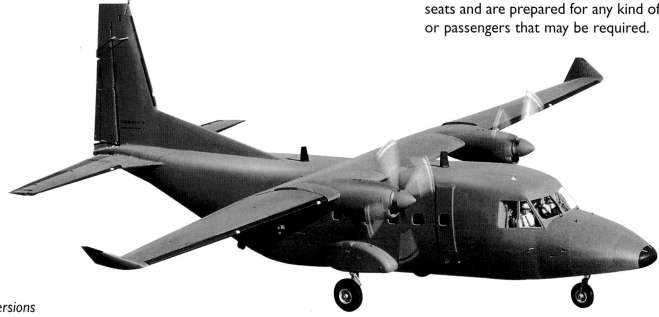

Versions

Apart from the its general support function, for which the Bendix land and meteorological evasion radar is very useful, specific variations of the plane have been designed. These included the options of photography via an opening in the fuselage that houses two Wild RC.10 cameras, seats and quality refurbishing of the interior for VIP travel, dropping loads from the air by parachute –LAPES, Low Altitude Parachute

> **MODERNIZED**
> The C-212 400 Series has been brought up to date with its in-flight equipment and customized technology, and has achieved noteworthy sales among traditional customers of Spanish airplanes.

Patrol

The Spanish SAR (Rescue and Assistance Service) squadrons that patrol and search using APS-128 radar detection needed to have the nose design changed and for additional fuel tanks to be added, and this inspired the Portuguese Air Force to order two "Patrol" units. Designed for monitoring fishing activity in Portuguese waters, they incorporate, among other

things, a search radar at the front and visibility radar on the sides, a microwave radiometer, a thermoradiometer, an IR/UV scanner, a long range navigation system, a special marine control communication system, a satellite data transmission system, an integrated photographic system, a searchlight, two observation bubbles and an aerial photography point.

Development

The individual needs of its different users and new advances in modern aeronautics meant that the first 100 Series could be followed by the 200 Series in 1978 with 250 additional kilograms of load. The 300 Series certified in 1987 with modified wings, nose and aviation instruments plus a larger cockpit, and the 400 Series that was presented at the Le Bouget show in 1997. This meant that the factory in Seville had to raise its production capacity.

400 Series

In accordance with the inherent characteristics of its design philosophy of a high wing that doesn't interfere with the loading bay capacity. A rear ramp that eases loading and unloading operations and strong wheels for operating on improvised runways. The excellent low-flying qualities of "Aviocar" have proved it an ideal model to be redesigned to confront the interesting

OPERATIVE
C-212s carry out all kinds of transport and supply tasks in support of other armed forces, noted for its outstanding efficiency in performing the tasks required of it.

FREIGHT
The hold of the C-212 was designed with the transportation of light vehicles and loads on palettes in mind, provided they do not exceed three metric tons.

expectations of the new century.

The most outstanding improvements are in the areas of operation, especially at high altitude and temperatures, and in crew comfort. The maximum weight not including fuel has gone up by 400 kilograms thanks to the new Allied Signal TPE-331-12JR-710C engine which supplies 925 extra horsepower, and has improved the take-off and flight capabilities in conditions of extreme heat.

Cockpit

The cockpit has been updated by substituting the old electromechanical instruments with the new Electronic Flight Instruments System (EFIS) made up of four screens which provide more reliable information. The traditional old engine instruments have been replaced with an Integrated Engine Data System (IEDS) that has two liquid crystal screens on which the data concerning the performance of the engine and the main systems of the plane (fuel, hydraulic, electrical, etc.) are displayed. The information is saved to memory for later analysis and to assist with maintenance work.

A Flight Management System (FMS) has also been installed, including a GPS receiver that uses the information supplied by sensors such as VOR, ADF and DME to plan navigation routes.

Transport

These vehicles are usually assigned to

Short Range Transport (SRT) tasks, which may often involve rapid, unexpected day or night missions transporting people or vehicals through unprepared territory. It has the ability to drop parachute troops day or night perform tactical support, medical evacuations by air, transporting VIPs, reinforcements and refuelling at low or high altitude in any kind of weather conditions, together with search and rescue missions.

The Spanish Air Force has performed these and other tasks whilst supporting the forces of United Nations (UN) in Namibia, and since the 15th July 1993 those of the

LAPES

The ability to release loads by means of the parachute extraction system means that "Aviocar" can accurately re-supply troops.

PARACHUTISTS

The C-212 of 72 squadron based at Alcantarilla (Murcia), are used for parachute training in the Spanish Air Force and Terrestrial Army.

North Atlantic Treaty Organization (NATO) in its efforts to hold the peace in the former Yugoslavia. On the 8th March 1994, whilst flying with the "Deny Flight" force, a Spanish T.12B of the 37th Wing was struck near its tail by a Serbian SA-7 anti-aircraft missile, causing 146 impacts and injuries to some of its occupants. However, it was retrieved after it had landed in Rijeka.

TAIL FIN

A large, high tail fin gives better performance quality during the flight and aids with the loading and unloading of people and material, as much on land as in aerial release.

UNDERCARRIAGE

The wheels are fixed and very sturdy, which allows the plane to land on improvised runways, thus enhancing its operative capabilities.

WING

The wing design and its location make loading easier and also increase the stability of the plane during its transport missions.

HOLD

It can be adapted for carrying personnel or material, and makes good use of the available space in a small vehicle, another important aspect of its muliti-purposfulness.

WEAPONS

Two small guns can be fitted onto the sides of the fuselage, just above the nose wheels, to support its operations with its own missile fire.

ENGINE

Equipped with four-blade propellers and an Allied Signal TPE-331-12-JR-701C turboprop engine that provides 1,850 horsepower, enough for carrying out the necessary transport tasks.

COCKPIT

The more advanced cockpit equipment has permitted the adaptation of the plane to each client's specific needs, and to the changing face of the aeronautics industry.

NOSE

Originally designed to house the secondary electronics equipment, the nose has grown over the years to accommodate such equipment as search radar and frequency receivers.

TECHNICAL DETAILS: C-212 Serie 400

COST:	13 million dollars	PROPULSION:	
SIZE:		Two Allied Signal TPE-331-12-JR-701 turboprop engines of 925 horsepower of continual energy	
Length	16.15 m		
Height	6.59 m	**FEATURES:**	
Wingspan	20.27 m	Maximum altitude	7,925 m
Wing surface	41 m²	Maximum speed	354 km/h
Flap surface	7.47 m²	Take-off distance	384 m for STOL operations
WEIGHT:			
Empty	3,800 kg	Maximum range	1.608 miles reduced to 500 miles for military operations with maximum load
Maximum	8,100 kg		
Maximum load	2,950 kg		
Fuel	2,040 kg		

The CN-235 is used by the Thai police for assistance work, by the Turkish Air Force (TUAF) for evacuating the wounded with 12 stretcher beds and two campaign surgeries in the hold, in tactical and logistical activities within the French Air Force's "Operation Turquesa" in Rwanda, by the Irish Air Corps for fishing vigilance, and for various other activities within the air forces of Spain, Brunei, Colombia, Chile, Ecuador, Botswana, Gabon, Morocco, Panama, Papua New Guinea, Saudi Arabia, the United Arab Emirates, the Republic of Korea and others. The CN-235 has proved itself to be a medium range transport airplane that offers the possibility of performing a wide range of military and civilian duties.

Project

In October 1979, the Spanish company Construcciones Aeronáuticas, SA (CASA) and the Indonesian PT Nurtanio, already having worked together on the C-212 "Aviocar", agreed to invest 80 million dollars into the development of a light transport plane; managed by their joint partners Airtec, based in Madrid. The original designs included both an elongated and an enlarged version of the C-212, but the one eventually chosen had a circular pres-

FUTURE

To meet CASA's requirements in the new century, the C-295 is an elongated and improved variation of the already known CN-235. It permits larger human or material cargoes, which raises the expectations of this Spanish two-engine plane.

MOROCCANS

A traditional buyer of Spanish military material, the Moroccan Air Force uses the CN-235 for many different transport activities, and paints the planes a sand color for camouflage.

surized fuselage and retracting undercarriage.

Development

Sharing the work among Spanish factories at Getafe, Seville and Cadiz and Bandung in Indonesia, the construction of the prototypes began in May 1981 and the official presentations of the finished products took place in Spain and Indonesia on 10th September 1983. CASA's ET-100 first took off on 11th November 1983, and the Indonesian PK-XNC did so the month after, starting a trial period in which several problems had to be rectified before obtaining the necessary certificate of airworthiness.

Factory production soon began, and on 19th August 1986 the first flight of a factory-produced 10 Series took place, to be followed by others until the 100 Series appeared in 1988. The letter M designated the planes destined for military duty, although there were several differences depending on the country of production as a result of disagreements between the two countries. After arduous testing and a complicated negotiation process, a contract was signed in 1991 with Tusas Aerospace Industries for the manufacture of many of the components and the last of the 52 units purchased by the Turkish Air Force, while the 300 Series ended up being short-listed by the Australian Air Force.

Maritime

In the early 1990s, CASA began developing the "Persuader" range, hoping to break into the market of maritime vigilance and patrol missions. In the first trial period a contract was signed with Ireland for the construction of two Maritime Vigilance (VM) planes. These went into service in 1995, controlling fishing, sea traffic and pollution, along with rescue operations. Fundamental for the latter is the Litton

KOREAN

The Republic of Korea's Armed Forces are good clients of the Spanish producer CASA, their Air Force (ROKAF) has twelve of their transport aircraft in their service.

APS504 search radar under the fuselage that integrates with the infrared detection system to optimize the search and identification facilities, and the operating console.

The PM (Maritime Patrol) model is more sophisticated and includes re-configurable universal consoles, which link through the TDMS tactical mission system that controls the operation of acoustic and non-acoustic sensors whose data is displayed on a 20 inch screen. It also has search radar providing ISAR and SAR images, a friend-foe interrogator, an ESM/ELINT tactile sensor, acoustic and electro-optic sensors, magnetic detectors, observation points, sonar buoy launchers and markers. Together with six under-wing supports that can hold different weapon systems, including anti-surface missiles that can perform anti-submarine or ship actions of short and medium range within a radius of 500 miles.

Dimensions and cost

The finished model measured 21.40 meters with an even longer wingspan, and a height of 8.17 meters. The cost of each individual unit was kept down to an accessible 16 million dollars. The military version weighs 8,800 kilograms on its own, and 16,500 when fully loaded and equipped, although this quantity, as shall be explained later, will be increased when the new C-295 comes into service.

Future

With over six hundred units sold, CASA has now produced an elongated version, first revealed at the 1997 Le Bourget show, which first flew in March 1998 and comes into service early in the year 2000 under the name of C-295. The Australian program to modernize its air fleet has already short-listed this plane, which maintains the same characteristics as its predecessor, with a larger cabin of 12.69 meters that allows for 50% more cargo, a reinforced wing to support the greater maximum weight of 23,200 kilograms, larger fuel tanks of 2,380 liters capacity, three fixing points of 300, 500 and 800 kilograms for the anchorage of weapons and systems on each half-wing, and an improved pressurization system.

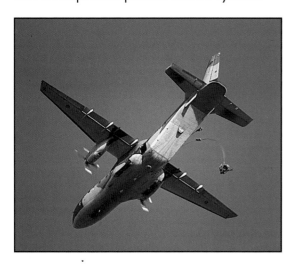

With a maximum load of 9,700 kg, or 69 fully-equipped soldiers, 27 stretcher beds with four nurses, or three light vehicles, the C-295 incorporates new technology into the configuration of the cabin, in which both FMS and IEDS have been installed. The undercarriage has been reinforced to support the extra weight. The engines have been replaced by Pratt & Whitney PW-127Gs, which move the six-bladed Hamilton Standard RF 568F propellers and provide 2,645 horsepower that can be temporarily

OPERATIVE

Because of its attributes and capabilities, the CN-235s of Wing 35 at Getafe in Spain are a basic element for the carrying out of complimentary transport tasks that are required by the Spanish Armed Forces.

MULTI-ROLE

Dropping parachutists wherever an Intervention Force is urgently needed or to take humanitarian aid to countries that have suffered a natural disaster are areas where the CN-235 has shown itself to be of value.

HOLD

Reconfigurable and adaptable to any form of transport, the hold offers a wide range of possibilities as shown by this configuration for evacuating up to 21 wounded with the assistance of medical personnel and equipment.

raised to 2,929 should one engine fail.

The plane can travel 780 miles without landing, cruises at 288 mph and can operate at altitudes up to 25,000 feet.

Multipurpose

With the capacity to take 48 parachutists 990 miles from their base, to evacuate 21 wounded from a point situated 1,420 miles from the departure point, to seek naval objectives for up to nine hours at distances up to 100 miles from base, or to take 2 tons of cargo 1,400 miles away and return in each case to its starting point, the CN-235 has lived up to the philosophy of its design and selected technical alterations by satisfying the criteria of sturdiness, operative capability, reliability and economy.

Military

Using materials specially designed to achieve a fine balance between the weight of the cargo and the structural weight, using a special reduced consumption and

easily maintainable power plant, and with the support of digital aviation to reduce breakdowns and incorporating surer and more efficient systems, the CN-235M stands out for a series of attributes that make it appropriate for several kinds of mission.

With a considerably wide cabin that permits the transport of an extensive variety of loads, short-distance landing wheels of low pressure in tandem, which allow operation on unpaved surfaces, and a double-door hydraulically operated rear ramp that offers easy access to the landing bay. This model is outstanding for its short take-off and landing (STOL) capabilities.

Its operational capacity is unlimited, and

PATROL

Employed by the Irish Air Corps, the CN-235 "Persuader" has been updated both internally and externally for maritime patrol, and has proved highly satisfactory.

it can release loads from very low altitude by means of its LAPES parachute extraction facility, transport any kind of logistic elements, quickly reconfigure for passenger transportation, adapt itself for parachutists, or serve as a platform for specific tasks such as electronic surveillance.

Configuration

The structure of the CN-235 has been designed to permit a wide range of accessory interchangeability, its projected time in service is 50,000 hours, and it is made with compound materials such as fiberglass and has a pressurized fuselage.

In front end is the cockpit that has been designed to comply with the needs of visi-

TECHNICAL CHARACTERISTICS CN-235M

COST:	16 million dollars	PROPULSION:	
DIMENSIONS:		2 General Electric CT7-9C turboprop engines of 1,750	
Length	21.40 m	horsepower which operate four-bladed Hamilton Standard 14-RF21	
Height	8.17 m	propellers	
Wingspan	25.81 m	**FEATURES:**	
Wing surface	59.10 m²	Maximum altitude	8,230 m
Flap surface	10.87 m²	Cruise speed	267 mph
WEIGHT:		Minimum speed	93 mph with flaps down
Empty military version	8,800 kg	Take off distance	512 m
Maximum	16,500 kg	Landing distance	376 m on land
Maximum load	6,000 kg	Maximum range	from 900 miles with 6 tons
Fuel	5,268 kg		of cargo to 2,670 miles
Cabin volume	22.82 m²		with 3.55 tons

PARACHUTISTS

The landing of personnel, by automatic or manual parachutes, is one of the tasks that the CN-235 serves for many of the military users that have opted for this medium capacity aeroplane (left photograph).

bility and ergonomics. Controlled by two pilots, it is digitized and has an Electronic Flight Instrumentation System (EFIS) and representation via five screens and an automatic pilot navigation system, flight director and OMEGA. From the cockpit the primary flight control systems are mechanically controlled. They are also duplicated in case of failure and the flaps are hydraulically activated.

Behind the cockpit is the hold, 9.65 m long, 1.88 m high, 2.7 m wide and with a volume of 43.24m2, which can be reached through the two small doors in the side of the fuselage or by a two-part ramp at the rear.

Above the hold are the wings which

MULI-PURPOSE

The loading facilities and the design of the hold allow for the easy undergoing of logistic or tactical air transportation (right photograph).

COCKPIT

The equipping of each CN-235 varies according to the client's needs, but includes all the necessary displays to reduce the workload of the pilot during flights.

hold the four fuel tanks, two main tanks and two auxiliaries that, when filled under pressure, can hold 5,268 liters. These feed a power plant made up of two General Electric CT7-9C turboprop engines that move the four-bladed Hamilton Standard 14RF-21 propellers and have a take off force of 1,750 horsepower, characterized by their cheap and simple maintenance and low fuel consumption; the one on the right is equipped with a propeller braking system that permits its use as a rescue unit, which means it does not need land support in order to operate in remote and unaided places.

Widely used for tactical transportation during the "Joint Endeavour" peace mission in Bosnia, the C-17 has shown that it should live up to the needs of the new century by transporting troops, equipment, humanitarian aid and so on to every corner of the globe.

This greatly reinforces the ample resources of Air Mobility Command (AMC) of the US Air Force which, among others, makes use of the C-130 "Hercules", C-141B "Starlifter" and C-5A/B "Galaxy" types, very useful for maintaining the rapid deployment of arms wherever their presence may be required.

«GLOBEMASTER» III

Designed to replace earlier models and improve the transportation capabilities of the US Air Force, the C-17 improves the quantity and quality of the deployment of all kinds of equipment, people and combat material.

HEAVY

Its capacity and potential has led to the C-17 being defined as a tactical form of transport designed for heavy transportation.

Requirements

The ongoing need to maintain the American fleet is made evident by the continual incorporation of new models and the processes of transformation and updating to which these vehicles are submitted.

Origins

A direct descendant of 1970s research with the YC-15 prototype that has recently re-started with a new series of studies, the air force's C-X program hoped to create a new airplane for heavy cargo transport. Of the two proposals made after the first series of studies, McDonnell Douglas's was selected on 28th August 1981 and development began in 1982, with the production contract being signed on 31st Decem-

ber 1985 for three prototypes. Manufacturing began at the beginning of November 1987.

The prototype was completed on 21st December 1990, the first test flight took place on 15th September of the next year, followed by a thorough capability verification program, the checking of attributes and evaluation of the results, including the introduction of a probe into the nose to transfer some of the parameters to the measuring station. Airframes T2 and T3 were presented in December 1991 and in the spring of 1992 underwent trials for such matters as the wear of the materials, impor-

SERVICE
C-17s are allocated to very specific programs. The first to receive this plane was Airlift Wing 437 in Charleston, South Carolina.

HOLD
The large hold is designed for housing heavy loads. The C-17 has been known to carry all kinds of vehicles, including tanks and helicopters.

tant for calculating the potential life span of a specific model.

Contract

The excellent results obtained by the lead plane constructed at the Long Beach plant in California, led to the series production of the model. The first C-17 was unveiled on 18th May 1992, although trials continued up until 1993.

Despite an initial requirement of 210 units, cuts in the budget limited the number to 120 in 1991 and to 40 in January 1994, with the current plan being for 120 units to be completed by the year 2004. However, it's not unlikely that future

or for use in trials for a version aimed at the civilian market.

Active

Currently serving in Airlift Wing 437 at their Charleston base, the first squadron was declared operational in January 1995 with 31 units being handed over up until the 1st of June 1997. By that date, the C-17 fleet had made over 50,000 hours flying time, and in May 1995 won the National Aeronautic Association of the United States' prestigious Collier Trophy.

Two more units were recently passed on to the 97 Air Mobility Wing at the Altur base in Oklahoma, and two further planes are destined for the McChord base in Washington and the Jackson base in Mississippi.

Advanced

During the trials to which the C-17 transport units (Class N, Group II, jet propelled) were submitted, 22 world records have been broken, including those for take-off and landing in less than 500 meters, reaching an altitude of 11,172 m with a cargo of 60,000 kilograms and taking a cargo of 73,039 kg up to 2,000 m.

The C-17 "Globemaster" costs about 100 million dollars to produce. It is 53.04 meters long and 16.79 meters high. When empty it weighs 122,016 kilograms and can carry a cargo weighing up to 77,292 kilograms, one of the greatest attractions

variants could increase the quantity of units going into service either for standard transport purposes, or for any other specialized needs that may occur at any given moment. The Marine Corps has recently given it a very positive evaluation, and it is quite possible that they might buy more units to complement their own "Hercules".

The production rate is currently 15 units a year. This is 45 days ahead of schedule, which has prompted McDonnell Douglas to manufacture two additional models which may be destined for abroad

TECHNICAL CHARACTERISTICS

COST:	aprox. 100 million dollars		PROPULSION:	
DIMENSIONS:			Four Pratt & Whitney F-111-PW-100 turbofan engines with a thrust	
Length	53,04 m		of 20,000 kg	
Height	16,79 m		**FEATURES:**	
Wing surface	353 m²		Maximum altitude	13.716 m
Aileron surface	11,83 m²		Cruising speed	Mach 0,74-0,77
Diameter of fuselage	6,85 m		Fully loaded approach	
WEIGHT:			speed	127 mph
Empty	122.016 kg		Take-off distance	512 m
Maximum	265.352 kg		Landing distance	470 m
Maximum load	77.292 kg		Operating range	5,220 miles
Internal fuel	102.624 l			

of this model that has enjoyed such continued success in the American Air Force.

Power

The four under-wing supported engines are high performance PW 2040 Pratt & Whitney turbofan engines designed by the air force as F117-PW-100 and each produces 40,440 pounds of thrust. The flow is reversible, as much as when airborne as on the ground, in the latter case helping to land when the plane is heavily loaded.

These low consumption engines are fed by four tanks built into the wings and the total structure has a capacity of up to 102,624 liters of JP8 or Jet A-1 fuel, making it a highly independent plane that, depending on the load, can travel around 5,220 miles. If necessary, it can receive extra fuel mid-flight via a probe just above and behind the cockpit.

Digital

Its advanced cockpit is outstanding for its digital flight controls, designed by General Electric, that are more accurate and have greater capacity than the previous ones. Only two pilots are needed to fly it, assisted by a third crewmember who performs complementary tasks such as managing the loading process. This is due to the use of advanced technology that can replace the navigator and flight engineer. The use of overhead sights to calculate parameters, four labor-saving and multi-role display screens and an integrated communication

control system, including hand operated sticks that facilitate control, but also free the eyes to be able to look at the instrument panels.

They also include systems such as the computer controlled cabin pressure, the Allied Signal GTCP331 integrated starter. The emergency fire control system and the equipment for automatically checking the state of the machinery, have been designed by General Dynamics.

Design

As the replacement for C-141Bs, the criteria applied to the C-17 should cover the expected needs of the first 25 years of the new century. Particularly emphasized has been the versatility, accessibility and easy maintenance of its components, using previously tested devices such as radios, inertials and meteorological radar and the use of jet engines that have already been well-used for commercial and

LANDING

The landing apparatus is built into the sides of the fuselage, the four large wheels permit landing on asphalt airstrips or improvised ones.

civilian purposes.

Certain novelties also appear on the aircraft, such as the small extensions to the wings, called 'winglets', that improve efficiency, the external flaps, the redesigned wings for low altitude flight, a large double door at the rear for loading and unloading, engines that deflect the flow upwards and backwards and the strong, retracting and low pressure nose undercarriage that permit operation on any land surface.

Capacity

Although its size and external design seem to reduce its overall capacity, the hold design permits the transportation of larger quantities than for example, the "Galaxy". It is 20.79 m long (not including the rear of the ramp), 5.49 m wide and 4.11 m high.

If configured for troop transport it can carry 186 people, or 102 people with 48 bunk beds, and has been known to transport an M-1 "Abrams" tank along with a 5-ton truck and a "Hummer" light vehicle, 6 light armored vehicles, 6 five-ton trucks, 2 AH-64 "Apache" helicopters and 3 OH-58D "Kiowa", 3 five-ton trucks and three 155 mm howitzers, or containers with the equipment and personnel to deploy a whole squadron of fighter-bombers. Alternatively, it can be transformed into a flying fuel tank.

Flexibility

THE COCKPIT

The C-17's cockpit includes all the latest technology and displays that make it much simpler for the pilot to fly.

The previous cargo capabilities, and the new additions to the revised version, give it an unrivalled flexibility in comparison with older models. It can be loaded with any kind of vehicle, material on palettes, logistic elements etc, and it can be reconfigured for aerial medical assistance, the release of parachutists from extreme heights thanks to the auxiliary respiratory system, low altitude parachute extraction (LAPES), container delivery (CDS) and combat palettes that can be extracted as the plane taxis. The C-17 can land on improvised runways such as deserts, highways and rapid deploy runways, such as those used by the marines, made out of aluminium strips.

HONOURED

Considered the most capable tactical and strategic aircraft of all, the C-17 "Globemaster" III notably improves the US Armed Forces' deployment capabilities.

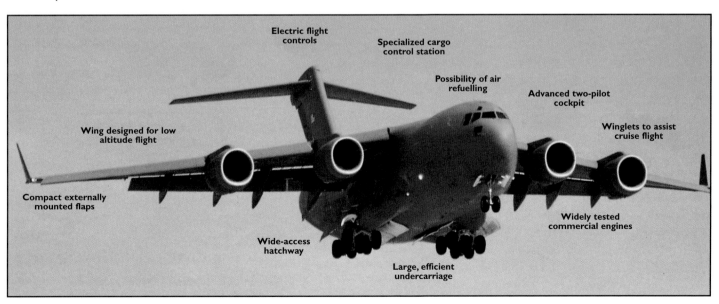

Electric flight controls

Specialized cargo control station

Possibility of air refuelling

Advanced two-pilot cockpit

Winglets to assist cruise flight

Wing designed for low altitude flight

Compact externally mounted flaps

Wide-access hatchway

Large, efficient undercarriage

Widely tested commercial engines

Known for its world-wide transportation of humanitarian aid and for its extensive role in the handling of military cargo, the C-130 "Hercules" is the definitive example. After almost half a decade of continued activity, and with 2,100 units constructed, it domonstrates how a good design can respond both to the demands of its time and to those of the future.

Adapted to a number of requirements, it is used as a cargo plane and in other activities such as aerial re-supplying, aerial vigilance, air-fire support, air rescue, fire control, electronic warfare, special operations, emergency airborne medical assistance, photographic surveillance, maritime patrol, missile deployment, meteorological investigation to name but a few. The military version has been acquired by sixty-four countries and has lent its services to some civil aviation companies.

> **BRITISH**
> The British C-130C Mk3, equipped with a platform for receiving extra fuel in mid-flight, is a good example of the capabilities of this aircraft that have given it the world-wide reputation it enjoys in the field of logistic transport.

Need

The increasing need for transport aircraft to replace the models that were used in the Second World War inspired the Tactical Command of the US Air Force to prepare the incorporation of new models in 1951. In September 1952, they teamed up with Lockheed to construct the prototype of a YC-130 whose inaugural flight took place on 23rd August 1954. 231 production units of the A version were manufactured up until 1959.

Service

A short while after, on 12th June, ver-

sion B entered service, including additional fuel tanks and higher powered engines; in April 1962 model E appeared, with a 5,145 liter fuel tank on each wing and a maximum weight for take-off of 70,310 kilograms. In March 1965, the first H was exported, with a cargo capacity of 19 tons or 70 parachutists.

After being updated in compliance with the needs of its clients and adapted to more varied purposes, Lockheed Martin

> **DEVELOPMENT**
> The C-130J, bought by the USA and the UK, is yet another advance on earlier versions and offers greater potential to incorporate the kind of technological advances that should keep this airplane in service until well into the new century.

has designed a more modern J version, which includes digital aviation instruments, more powerful engines and structural changes that will enable it to meet the challenges of the 21st century. It is now capable of flying further and with a larger cargo capacity than earlier versions, yet at the same time it is easier to operate and maintain.

Specialized

Mainly used as a general cargo plane that transports all types of containers, light tanks, vehicles, different weapons, troops and parachutists. The "Hercules" as it is commonly known, has been modified to satisfy the varying requirements of the air forces it supplies.

Several models have outstanding features. The C-130-30 has an extended fuselage that lifts the cargo capacity to a possible 92 parachutists. The AC-130 "Spectre" has 7.62, 20, 25, 40 and 105 mm guns and a guided firing system that allows it to support surface vehicles. The EC-130 "Compass Call" is equipped with an electronic system that can interrupt the communication, control and steering of enemy planes. The KC-130 has internal tanks and a system of transferring fuel mid-flight which can refuel any other kind of aircraft. The MC-130 "Combat Talon II" is designed to support the missions of the Special Forces. The VC-130 transports VIPs. The EC-130V uses revolving AN/APS-145

ASSISTANCE

The cargo capacity, the navigation instruments and the radio are amongst the aspects that make "Hercules" an ideal machine for humanitarian aid missions all around the world.

MULTI-ROLE

Wherever a group of fighter planes is operating, one or more C-130s also need to be sent to transport the support equipment and to take fuel for mid-flight supply.

radar for aerial vigilance. The EC-130 ABCCC becomes a battle command and control center thanks to a special container situated in the hold. The LC-130 is equipped to land and take-off in snow and ice. "Eagle Claw" boasts retrorockets that allow it to land in a football stadium. AEH is equipped with all that is necessary to care for the wounded. HC-130 is equipped for the rescue of retreating troops... and there are still over a hundred other variants that could be mentioned.

Features

The most widely used variant, the C-130H, has a medium size four-engine design that permits it to perform an astounding variety of tasks, at either regular or improvised air bases. The classic design is easily recognizable for the wide diameter of the fuselage. High on the front part of the plane is the air-conditioned cockpit that accommodates the pilot, co-pilot and the flight engineer. Behind that is the hold, reconfigurable according to each particular mission, and is reached by passing through a two-part hatchway (the lower part doubles as a ramp). There is also a side door for the passengers to board.

In a high position, so as not to interfere with loading, is the wing, which incorporates two turboprop engines on each segment. The high rear tail-fin is designed to improve the chances of operating on unusual surface types. The three pairs of hydraulically retracting landing wheels allow operation on semi-prepared runways

and can turn at a radius of 11.28 m.

It is equipped with diverse communication systems, either Westinghouse AN/APN-241 radar or the newer Sperry, an AN/ARN-152 (V) microwave landing system. A Doppler AN/APN-232 navigator, a detector that warns against approaching land, a flight data recorder, are among the many other features fitted to this aircraft.

Advanced

Updated by several users, one of the most advanced variations is that of Constucciones Aeronáuticas, SA (CASA), who are currently working with Lockheed on an assignment for the Spanish Air Force (EA). As a result of the increasing number of multinational support missions and the fact that the plane has been in operation for a quarter of a century, a modernisation schedule has been programed that will last until the year 2000. This will include navigation system improvements with a new inertial system and GPS, the updating of the flight

ELONGATED

With a longer fuselage to permit transportation of larger and heavier loads, the elongated "Hercules" is used by Wing 31 of the Spanish Air Force and has been given the number 31-01 in memory of a plane that crashed in the Canary Islands.

OPERATIVE

The cargo capacity, wide range of transport options, the long distances it can cover, a long life span and remarkable reliability are some of the features that users of "Hercules" have praised.

control systems with a new computer and the incorporation of liquid crystal display screens. In addition, the incorporation of new UHF/VHF/HF radios with secraphonic systems that make it harder for communication to be intercepted. The replacement of the wings and APUs of some units, and the installation of a self-protection system made up of a warning system, decoy launchers and the shielding of the cockpit against light weapons, is also underway.

Super «Hércules»

With seven modified units undergoing trial, this new generation variant, called C-130J, has been ordered by the United States, Great Britain, Australia and Italy. Sixteen months after it was initially expected, the British Royal Air Force put the first unit into operation in October 1998.

Despite the initial delivery delays, due to the need to validate the new additions and to make certain adaptations to comply with expectations, the C-130J, compared with its 1991 version, has much more

powerful AE 2100D3 engines which produce 4,591 horsepower each, has more efficient six-blade Dowty Aerospace R391 propellers which improve the range and speed, has a flight cabin equipped with digital technology derived from that used in hunter aircraft, including liquid crystal and holographic display screens. It has been equipped with Kevlar and ceramic panels to protect the crew from light weapon impact, and has also been designed to be flown by pilots wearing night-vision goggles.

The advances made in materials and

FEATURES

The recent modification of the C-130 is the J version, which can take off and land in limited spaces, as well as its bigger engines and capacity.

LANDING

Although it is quite capable of landing on improvised runways, the runways of airports and air bases normally serve for the C-130 to carry out its transportation duties.

engine efficiency in the last few years, have resulted in this aircraft's increase in endurance by 40%, as well as an increase in crusing altitude by 40%. The top speed has also been increased by 21%; but at the same time the fuel consumtion has incresed as well. They are expected either to purchase the standard version, or the lengthemed C-130J-30 as a replacement for older models. Other countries have expressed an interest in the new model and should shortly start putting in their bids, particularly if other programs do not work out, such as the multinational FLA (Future Large Aircraft).

TAIL FIN

There is a large tail fin on the rear end of the "Hercules" to increase its flight potential. It is situated high enough so as not to affect the operations that use the rear ramp.

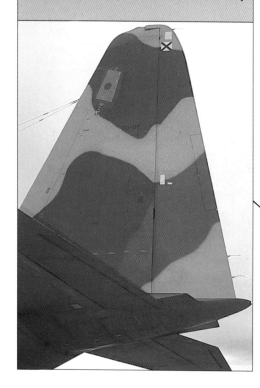

ENGINES

The plane is driven by four Allison T56-A-15 turboprop engines, which offer 18,032 horsepower and activate constant speed four-blade Hamilton Standard 54H60 propellers.

HOLD

The hold capacity permits a wide range of configurations for material or human transport, or both, and can then be reconfigured to another purpose thanks to the floor with rollers and hooks on the walls and ceiling.

MAIN UNDERCARRIAGE

Built into the side of the fuselage, the wheels are of low pressure, which permits operation on unprepared runways and the transportation of heavy cargoes.

COCKPIT

Two pilots and a navigator, complemented by a flight assistant, are in control of the tasks assigned to these transport airplanes.

PILOTING

The cockpit contains all the instruments needed for the monitoring of flight parameters, somewhat obsolete these days as a result of new technological breakthroughs that have taken the place of such equipment.

RADAR

The black nose is a dome that covers the small radar that supports the flight operations, offering information about the terrain, altitude and weather.

UNDERCARRIAGE

At the front of the plane, there are two small wheels that help move the plane when it taxis on the ground.

TECHNICAL CHARACTERISTICS: C-130H

COST:	30 millones de dólares	External fuel	10.600 l
DIMENSIONS:		**PROPULSION:**	
Length	29.79 m	Four Allison T56-A15 turboprop engines with a potential 4,508	
Heigh	11.66 m	horsepower that move constant speed four-blade Hamilton	
Wingspan	40.41 m	Standard 54H60 propellers	
Wing surface	162.12 m²	**FEATURES:**	
Flap surface	31.77 m²	Maximum altitude	8,075 m
Hold surface	39.5 m²	Maximum speed	350 mph
WEIGHT:		Time to reach 6,000 m	22 minutes
Empty	34,686 kg	Take-off distance	1.219 m
Maximum	79,380 kg	Landing distance	457 m
Maximum load	22,597 kg	Range with 18-ton cargo	2,160 miles
Internal fuel	25,816 l		

MULTI-ROLE

Designed as the principal anti-submarine element on aircraft carriers, the "Viking" has developed towards other purposes such as attacking ships on the surface, electronic surveillance, transportation or refuelling at sea – a very wide range of capabilities indeed.

Designed to serve as the main anti-submarine airplane giving protection to US aircraft carriers and escort units, the S-3 "Viking" has shown throughout its ser-

CAPABLE

The design, equipment and features of the S-3B make it a sophisticated means of detecting surface and underwater vessels, at the same time guaranteeing their own survival by detecting them with enough time to respond appropriately.

vice of over twenty years that is quite capable of serving not only in this capacity, but to perform several other functions that support aircraft operating from ships.

Operational

Midway through the 1970s the need became apparent for a replacement for the S-2 "Tracker", responsible for anti-submarine warfare (ASW) on US aircraft carriers.

After studying five initial proposals, Lockheed's design was finally chosen. 461 million dollars were granted for the funding of the project.

Contractor

As the main contractors, Lockheed was responsible for the construction of the fuselage, the installation of the avionic systems, the assembly of the equipment and the final trials, and also worked with companies like Vought, who manufactured the wings, tail unit, wheels and undercarriage assembly. Univac provided the computer that linked the sensors, and other companies supplied the lesser accessories.

Due to the urgency of the project, the first prototype took to the air on 21st January 1972. Eight test models had been completed within the next year, so the configuration process was surprisingly fast. In February 1974, the US Navy received the first completed aircraft.

Operative

VS-41 Training Squadron, whose Naval Air Station is at North Island, California received these first aircraft. They were able to show their operational potential at sea when ten planes were deployed on the USS "Kennedy" in 1975.

In mid 1978, 187 units had been constructed, and the production line at Burbank was closed. However, Lockheed's engineers had already thought up ways of developing the earlier project to further satisfy the

ELECTRONIC

Known as the ES-3A, the electronic version of the "Viking" takes advantage of its fuselage to contain an element specialized in supporting naval and aerial missions.

MULITI-PURPOSE

The ES-3A carry out electrical signal surveillance tasks, which identify possible enemies and work towards their elimination, but are also involved in the re-supplying and refuelling of other planes.

requirements of the marines. They did this by widening its capabilities and making it more powerful.

The 1980 program to produce a new model was inspired by WSIP (Weapon System Improvement Program), and on 18 August 1981 work began on the transformation of a plane into the standard S-3B.

On the 13th September 1984, the first test aircraft took to the air. And after the trial process, on 28th April 1986, an agreement was reached for the manufacture of 22 modernization kits that would be fitted to the airframes at NAS Cecil Field in Florida.

The first renovated models were ready by December 1987, and after ordering new kits, three squadrons of the Atlantic fleet had been remodeled by the end of 1991. In the same way, 38 of the Pacific Fleet's planes stationed at NAS North Island were also redeveloped.

Development

At the same time, at the beginning of the 1980s, the US-3A variant had also been proposed, in which the aviation system had already been replaced to configure a liaison and light transport model, and the KS-3A, designed to refuel aircraft at sea. Eventually, it was the latter of the two that received the anti-submarine apparatus supplied with under-wing "Sargent-Fletcher" containers that allowed the plane to pass some of its own fuel on to others.

The development contract of a long range electronic surveillance version, using technology introduced in January 1991 that is able to detect objects well beyond the horizon, was signed in March 1988. This plane first flew on 15th May 1991, and since 1992, 16 aircraft have been constructed, under the name of ES-3A, out of old frames. These used a simplified version of the operating system used in the EP-3E "Orion" and included three AN/AYK-14 data-processing computers, an ESM AN/ALR-76 system, AN/APS-137 radar, data coding link 11, an AN/APX-76 friend- or-foe interrogator, FLIR OR-236 infrared vision and other items that turned

COMPACT

The fact that the "Viking" has folding wings and tail helps reduce the space needed to fit it into a packed hangar or into the decks of aircraft carriers.

MOVEMENT

During maintenance work, which is performed in the large holds of aircraft carriers, we can see the small stairway that leads the pilot and his assistants onto the plane.

the planes into excellent transmissions receivers of from either naval or land units.

Description

With some 130 models being used in different Navy units, the "Viking" responds to the requirements of seaborne anti-submarine and land detection, and its size and characteristics are ideal for such tasks, particularly when backed up by the more powerful P-3 "Orion".

Configuration

Two turbofanes General Electric TF34-GE-2 Two General Electric TF34-GE-2 jet engines produce 8,300 kilograms of thrust, allowing the plane to reach a maximum speed of 500 mph, enough to carry out the kind of tasks usually required of it, which tend to be slow speed, low flying missions. The engines are encased under each of the wings, very close to the fuselage, and they can either be fuelled from their integrated tanks or from the underwing ones, and they are given back-up by an additional jet engine, extra fuel can be administered via a retractable probe situated above the cockpit.

The design is noted for its rounded sha-

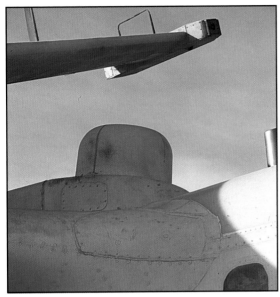

pe which creates the space needed in the cockpit for the two pilots to work, with a tactical area for systems operation and a bay where the weapons and detection equipment are stored. As an emergency provision, the four crewmembers sit on McDonnell Douglas Escapac IE-I ejector seats. The small but sturdy undercarriage assists operations in connection with aircraft carriers, there is a hook on the underside of the tail and both the wings and tail fin can be folded, thus reducing the space it occupies when in hangars or holds.

The large, thick wings and tail stabilisers substantially improve the plane's ability to patrol the seas and to pursue submarines and ships.

Power

Specially equipped for carrying out complicated missions, the S-3 incorporates an AN/AYS-I Proteus acoustic signal pro-

cessor, an IBM AN/UYS computer that works in conjunction with a Sander AN/OL-320/AYS data processor. An ESM electronic support system including IBM AN/ALR-76, Texas Instruments AN/APS-137 (V) I radar with high resolution inverse synthetic lens. A sonar buoy launcher that works with a Cubic AN/ARS-4 system, a Goodyear AN/ALKE-39 interference rocket launcher. The latest communication and navigation equipment and an extendible spar that includes MAD that can detect magnetic abnormalities.

With all of this, the sensor operator and the tactical co-ordinator who sits behind the pilot can locate the target and enter combat with an arsenal made up of 324 mm light torpedoes, bombs, rocket launchers, anti-surface missiles, mines and nuclear depth charges. All these are carried in the bomb bay or in the under-wing supports.

TECHNICAL CHARACTERISTICS:

COST:	45 million dollars	External fuel	2.272 l
DIMENSIONS:		**PROPULSION:**	two General Electric TF-34-GE-2 jet engines with a thrust of 4,150 kg
Length	16.26 m		
Height	6.93 m	**FEATURES:**	
Wingspan	20.93 m	Maximum altitude	12,200 m
Wing surface	55.74 m²	Maximum speed	500 mph
WEIGHT:		Take-off distance	807 m
Empty	10,954 kg	Maximum range	3,651 miles
Maximum	21,592 kg		
Internal fuel	7,192 l		

The need for maritime vigilance, submarine pursuit, sea traffic control and sea rescue were some of the reasons why European aeronautic manufacturers began working on special projects to design airplanes for such missions. Most capable and enthusiastic were the French "Atlantic/ Atlantique" group based in Germany, Italy, Pakistan and France itself, and the British based "Nimrod".

French

Derived from the 1958 project that won the right to supply NATO with a new maritime patrol plane, the "Atlantic" ALT1 was put into production by the international consortium SEC-BUT (Société d'Etude et de Construction du Breguet Atlantic) and purchased by four NATO member countries, which along with the three aforementioned countries also included Holland.

Updating

Having already clocked over a million years of fleet operation, in May 1984 the French government gave the go-ahead for production of an improved series called ALT2 "Atlantique", of which all 30 units are already in operation, the original target of 42 was never reached for budget reasons.

NEW GENERATION

The 3 series Atlantique will receive newer and more complete detection, analysis and classification equipment for locating and destroying threats from on or under the water's surface, and will remain in service until the third decade of the next century.

ANTI-SURFACE

The French Atlantique has received the necessary equipment to operate with AIM-39 "Excocet" anti-surface missiles, turning it into a lethal surface vessel fighter plane.

The Italians, who wish to replace their fleet with a more modern design, have updated "Atlantic" with a Thomson-CSF Iguane radar and a GEC Avionics AQS-902 acoustic system, while the Germans have started modifying their own airframes and avionics by incorporating Texas Instruments APS-134 (V) radar and installing Loral Rapport ESM containers on the

edges of the wings to create their new KWS model.

Dassault Aviation recently announced that they are working on a third generation "Atlantic" that shall be called ALT3 and will use an airframe produced by SEC-BAT incorporating new mission avionics, Allison AE2100H engines and six-blade Dowty propellers, coded data links, more powerful weaponry, a refueling platform and various sensors related to anti-submarine and anti-surface work, and it will only require 8 crew members to operate it.

Design

Completely made of metal, the fuselage

SHARED WORKLOAD

The display screen operators and detection teams of the French Atlantique are supplied with several machines for carrying out their identification duties, so important for the successful accomplishment of a mission.

GERMAN

To carry out marine patrol over the turbulent North Atlantic seas, with its shallow depth and complex fjords, the German Atlantic has advanced orientation systems that permit the detection and elimination of either surface or submergible vessels.

is made up of the pressurized upper section that houses the crew, and a lower section containing the 9-meter weapons bay that can store 2.5 tons of arms. The wing has been designed to reach economical cruising speeds on long range patrols and there is a glass cabin on the nose where a lookout can be seated.

The flight crew is made up of the pilot, co-pilot and mechanic, along with nine crew members who verify the data obtained by the sensors on four special consoles. From here they can also control the equipment, which includes Thomson-CSF Iguane surface discovery radar fixed into a retractable observation sphere under the fuselage, inferred explorers, an electronic support mechanisms container, a Sadang data processing system, an Alkan sonar buoy launcher, thomson-TRT 35 cameras and a MAD Crouzaet magnetic abnormality detector, which allows for the detection of surface and underwater vessels.

Once detected, they can be attacked with the eight 324 mm Mk46 "Murene" light torpedoes, "Magic" air-to-air missiles, mines or the Aeroespatiale AS-37 "Martel" and AIM-39 anti-surface missiles, enough to counterattack any threat from under or on the water.

British

The need to substitute the Avro "Shackleton" led the Royal Air Force to select the British Aerospace "Nimrod" as its ideal successor for marine patrol missions. In

June 1964, under the name of project HS.802, work began on the design of a new plane. Two prototypes were developed from the incomplete frames of "Comet" Mk 4C civilian airplanes. The second of which first flew on 23rd May 1967 with four Rolls-Royce Rb.168 Spey jet engines.

NIMROD 2000

The logical evolution of earlier models, the Nimrod is a marine patrol plane noted for its turbo powered engines, increase it's speed and the area it can cover, and can also carry a greater load, including a heavy arsenal of weapons.

Acquisition

The contract for 38 models went ahead and on 28th June 1968 the first production unit took off. This was sent to the Maritime Training Operations Unit at St.Mawgan on the 2nd October 1969. In February 1972 the manufacture of those planes destined for squadrons OCU 42, 120, 201, 203, 206 and 236 was completed, and an additional order was made for 8 Nimrod MR MkI that would be used as reserves.

The units of this second order started flying from 1974, and they were used simultaneously to test new avionics and sensor systems. A prototype of this reconfigured format made its first flight in June 1976. The first operational Mark II aircraft was completed at woodford on the 13 th of February 1979, on the 23 rd of August 1979 a contract was signed for the conversion of the remaining nimrods T6 Mk.2 aircraft although eventually 35 planes were updated.

Falklands

With mid-air refueling capability, underwing supports for air-to-air missiles etc, they were a quick solution for the control of surface vessels, electronic data capture and the rescue of air crews that had landed in the sea during the Falklands Conflict of 1982.

EXCLUSIVE

Used only by the British Air Force, the Nimrod has a Searchwater radar antenna fitted above the cockpit and an air refuelling tube.

The Loral ESM containers on the edges of the wings, were added to the updated Mk2, which was completed in 1985. To maintain its capacity against threats in the future, a more powerful adaptation was announced in 1997. The remodelling of 21 Nimrod 2000, or MRA.4, was begun, to be completed in the year 2000 with the incorporation of all the latest electronic and systems technology of recent years. Among these are a two-seater cockpit, similar to those used in the Airbus, a Searchwater 2000MR radar, BMW/Rolls-Royce BR710 jet engines and the Racal Defensive Aid Sub-System.

Details

The Nimrod incorporates a spacious fuselage with a non-pressurized lower section in which the radar is housed. A 4.78 m long armaments bay with some equipment and systems and an upper section where the twelve man crew operates.

Four Rolls Royce 168-20 Mk250 jet engines are situated on the wings. They produce enough thrust for the aircraft to travel at speed in excess of 500 mph. Even with three engines shot down, there is still enough power from the remaining engine to keep the aircraft airborne. The two outer engines can reverse their trust, so that the plane can land on short runways.

The Thorn-EMI Searchwater radar is fitted onto the large nose, this can locate sur-

SPECIALITY
Some of the aspects that differentiate the Nimrod from other vehicles are the electronic warfare systems at the ends of the wings, the engines built into the wings and fuselage and the large internal hold.

SEARCH
Built into the right wing of the Nimrod is a powerful searchlight, which allows exploratory missions to take place even in the most adverse lighting conditions.

face and airborne objects. Above the cockpit is a mid-air refueling probe, this enables this plane to patrol for as long as 19 hours. The two containers on the sides hold the ESM Loral 1017A electronic support mechanisms, complemented by the passive Thomson-CSF attached to the end of the tail fin. The tail is the magnetometer of the Emerson ASQ-10A magnetic abnormality detector and at the back there is the active and passive sonar buoy launchers of various types. Toghether with the Australian BARRA, the Canadian TANDEM, the British CAMS the American SSQ-41 and SSQ-53 that send data to the AQS-901 acoustic processing system.

Once the target has been located, the plane has the option of using the Marconi "Sting Ray" anti-submarine torpedo, depth charges, mines or AGM-84 "Harpoon" anti-surface vessel missiles. To which can be added AIM-9 "Sidewinder" air-to-air missiles, free-fall bombs or cluster bombs. All of which are carried in the bay or in the containers situated on the wings.

EQUIPMENT

Under the pilot's cabin is the observation position the infrared sensor, air intake to the cooling system and the front undercarriage.

ENGINES

The Rolls Royce Tyne Rty.20 Mk21 turboprop engines of 6,100 hp are contained in the same casing into which part of the Messier-Bugatti undercarriage is folded after take-off.

COCKPIT

The cockpit is where the pilot works alongside the co-pilot and engineer who are not only responsible for the movement of the plane, but also for the detection systems that advise them on the best routes to take on exploratory missions.

14RADAR

The antenna of the Thomson-CSF Iguane exploratory radar is held in this retractable bubble, and covers a full 360° range. It quickly spots any object on the sea surface, even those as small as the small periscopes used by submarines.

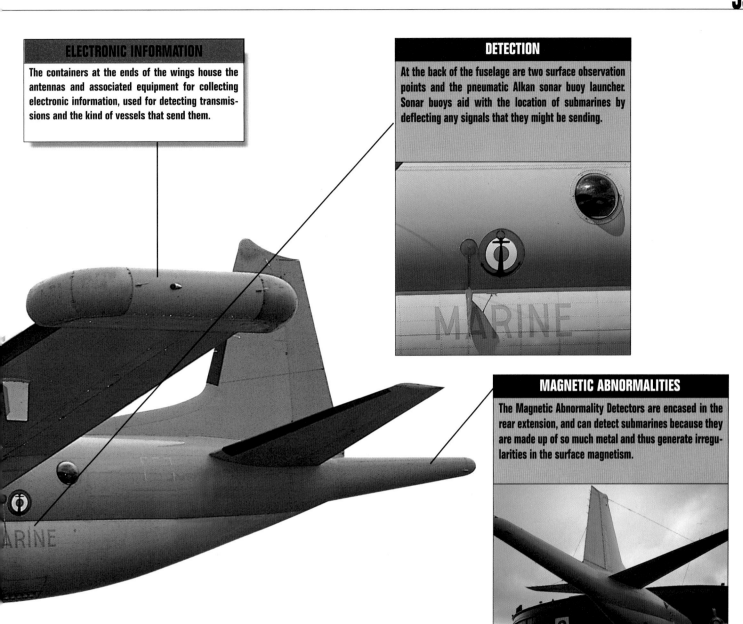

ELECTRONIC INFORMATION

The containers at the ends of the wings house the antennas and associated equipment for collecting electronic information, used for detecting transmissions and the kind of vessels that send them.

DETECTION

At the back of the fuselage are two surface observation points and the pneumatic Alkan sonar buoy launcher. Sonar buoys aid with the location of submarines by deflecting any signals that they might be sending.

MAGNETIC ABNORMALITIES

The Magnetic Abnormality Detectors are encased in the rear extension, and can detect submarines because they are made up of so much metal and thus generate irregularities in the surface magnetism.

TECHNICAL CHARACTERISTICS

	ATLANTIQUE	NIMROD MK2
COST:	100 million dollars	120 million dollars
DIMENSIONS:		
Length	33.63 m	38,63 m
Height	11.30 m	9,06 m
Wingspan	37.46 m	35 m
Wing surface	120.34 m²	197,2 m²
Flap surface	26.42 m²	
Internal work		
surface	155 m²	196,4 m²
WEIGHT:		
Empty	25,600 kg	39.000 kg
Maximum	46,200 kg	87.090 kg
Maximum external cargo	3,500 kg	--
CTotal weapon cargo	6,000 kg	6.120 kg
Internal fuel	23,120 lts	48.780 lts

PROPULSION:	two Rolls-Royce Tyne turboprop engines engines of 6,100 horsepower thrust per unit	Four Rolls Royce Spey RB.168-20 Mk250 jet engines of 5,507 kg thrust per unit
FEATURES:		
Maximum altitude	9,145 m	12.660 m
Low flying speed	389 mph	555 mph
Economy speed	333 mph	472 mph
Patrol speed	189 mph	222 mph
Take-off distance	1.840 m	1.400 m
Landing distance	1.500 m	800 m
Operational range	900 miles plus 5 hours of exploration time	1,200 miles plus 5 hours of exploration time
Maximum range	5,445 miles	5,556 miles

Updated

Thus, in January 1975 the first Update variant, with new avionics, unvield. It also possessed more advanced software, a tactical display screen, Omega navigation system and an improved acoustic processor. Update number 2 came in 1976, with its Infrared Detection System and Sonar Buoy Reference System. Those produced after 1977, such as the 13 that were for the Dutch Marines, could fire "Harpoon" missiles.

A new Proteus IBM UYS-1 acoustic processor, a more potent sonar buoy receptor, an advanced APU system and greater comfort for the crew are some of the improved characteristics of update number 3, which came into production in 1984 and was maintained up until the late 80s. Some models have since been updated and converted into this model, under the name of IIIR.

With continued activity in observing Soviet Union submarine and ship activity during the 1970s and 1980s, the P-3 "Orion" played an active role in the search for surface targets, the co-ordination of movements, aerial surveillance and rescue missions during the Gulf War, deplyment and organization of squadrons during flight.

> **PATROL**
>
> P-3s can be adapted for particular missions, which is the main reason why nearly 650 units have been built for use in 14 different countries, and it is expected that many of these will be modernized so that they can continue in service.

Need

In 1958, with a variant of the commercial vehicle Electra, Lockheed won the US Navy's order for an anti-submarine plane. The prototype flew on 19th August 1958. On 25th November 1959, the YP-3A with avionics did likewise, and in August 1962 the P-3A, with similar qualities entered service and was maintained by the Navy until November 1978.

Midway through the 70s a B variant was completed with Allison T-56-A-14 turboprop engines, of which 124 went to the US Navy, 5 to Norway, 5 to New Zealand and 10 to Australia. The C Variant first flew on 18th September 1968, equipped with new sensors and equipment linked by a digital Univac computer. The capacity of these sensors meant that between 1969 and 1978, 143 of these units were incorporated into the anti-submarine wings of the US Marines, as soon as they went into service, possibilities of updating them were already being investigated.

> **GROUP 22**
>
> The Spanish Orions are used by Group 22 of the Air Force at Morón Base, and their main responsibility is the vigilance of the Strait of Gibraltar and the merchant routes that connect Europe and Africa.

Transformation

80 old airframes were scheduled for modification in 1991 into the standard Update IV, although financial problems put an early end to the project. However, what did happen, born from the deficiencies observed during the Gulf war, was the AIP (Anti-surface Warfare Improvement Program), for which the Unisys Government Group worked on improving their 68 P-3C Update IIIs, with new sensors, satellite communication, data processing and handling and systems for armaments and survival against threats from beyond the horizon.

In its place appeared a highly advanced

variation called P-7A LRAACA (Long-Range Air ASW-Capable Aircraft) with General Electric turboprop engines of 6,000 hp, new plasma display screens and an improved control systems. However, its entry into service was delayed due to a prolonged decision-making process in which a variant of the Boeing 757 was considered as an alternative.

> **UPDATED**
>
> Despite being quite dated, the electronic capacity of the P-3 has been modernized by continuous improvement programs that should keep the plane in service until the second decade of the new century.

Users

Although the updating process has been continued, the budget problems in some countries have made it more difficult for them than it was for the US Navy, who have acquired 555 models of this patrol plane and still has 424 in operation. Spain uses two P-3As that it received from the US in Group 22 at Morón, along with five P-3Bs that it bought from Norway. Several modifications have been made to these planes which are now almost ready to re-enter service. Each unit costing over six and a half million dollars to update. The Argentinean Arma-

> **CAPACITY**
>
> The fact that the US Marines still use more than four hundred P-3 "Orion" in submarine and surface detection operations suggests that this airplane is well suited to such tasks, and its potential has always been the subject of admiration.

da patrols with six P-3s, and uses the other two as a source of spare parts. Canada has its own variant that is called CP-140 "Aurora". Chile uses 10 UP-3A, Japan has advanced versions of model C. Iran received some P-3Fs and still uses 5 of them as surveillance planes. The Korean Marines have received 8 P-3Cs since 1994. Greece and Turkey have some second-hand ones. Norway and Holland fly updated P-3Cs. Australia is improving some of its own P-3C under Project Air 5276 into the standard AP-3C, and has transformed 3 P-3Bs into training aircraft TAP-3. Portugal operates 6 P-3Ps and even Great Britain has considered buying some to replace the Nimrod. In total, some 650 models exist in 14 countries.

Platform

The successful sales of the P-3 "Orion" are due to the adequate combination of a well-used platform with the installation of equipment that has been adapted to hard threats. Permitting the updating of its capabilities in a fairly uncomplicated way and facilitating the incorporation of new technology that notably improves its chances in air-to-surface combat.

Autonomy

An outstanding facet of this plane is its independent nature when doing patrol work, due to its fuel tank built into the fuselage and another four in the wings. When on patrol in search of a target, it can fly by using only two or three of its

four Allison T56-A-14 turboprop engines. These each produce 4,910 hp and use Hamilton Standard 54H60-77 propellers. On such patrols, it tends to spend a lot of time just above sea level to help in its target search. The power of its propulsion unit is quite remarkable. In fact, an "Orion" broke the world record for a turboprop flying in a straight line when it reached a speed of 483 mph.

Equipped with such items as a stove, fridge and dining room, it is very comfortable for long missions, the fuselage is sufficiently large to house a crew of ten. These are divided into a group of three who are responsible for flight direction from the cockpit, and a group of seven that uses the consoles and operates the different weapon systems, all working in a pressurized and air conditioned environment.

Complex

The standard equipment that the US Navy uses tends to vary according to different modification projects, but includes

DESIGN
Developed from a civilian aircraft, the "Orion" has a particularly attractive design, and moreover, can be adapted to serve a wide variety of purposes.

TURBOPROP
Four powerful Allison T56-A-14 turboprop engines propel Hamilton Standard rotors. Yet, the "Orion" is capable of performing patrol missions by only using two of them, thus reducing fuel consumption.

the Proteus AN/ASQ-114 central digital processor for controlling sensor data and then sending it to the four tactical co-ordination display screens (with two acoustic and two non-acoustic sensors). These work with the AN/AYA-8 data processor to calculate the best options for counterattacking the enemy. Among the sensors is a Texas Instruments AN/APS-117 surface radar, with arials on the nose and tail that permit 360° scanning, thus improving the chances of identifying targets. An AN/ASQ-81 Magnetic Abnormality Detector is situated as far as possible from the plane's body so as to be able to monitor the surface more easily for the evidence of submarines. An AN/ASQ-64 submarine abnormality detector, a passive infrared FLIR day and night vision system, a AN/APX-72 friend-foe identifier, a LTN-72 inertial navigation system, AN/APN-194 altimetric radar and AN/ASW-31 automatic flight control system are also used.

In operation, it has a central launcher, some of whose modules can be recharged from within the aircraft, this uses activating cartridges to launch signals and sonar buoys that help detect underwater objects through the incorporated hydrophones. These signal the areas where it is supposed that the targets are with marine markers Mk 3A and Mk 7, that either color the air or emit smoke signals which can be observed from long distances. They are supported by an electronic combat mechanism to locate any transmission.

TECHNICAL DETAILS: P-3C

COST:	60 million dollars		Fuel	34.826 l
SIZE:			**PROPULSION:**	Four Allison T56-A-14 turboprop
Length	35.61 m			engines that produce 4,910 horsepower
Height	10.27 m			per unit and operate four-rotor Hamilton
Wingspan	30.37 m			Standard 54H60-77 propellers of constant
Wing surface	120.77 m²			speed
Cabin surface	61,13 m²		**FEATURES:**	
			Maximum altitude	8,625 m
WEIGHT:			High altitude speed	457 mph
Empty	27,890 kg		Patrol speed	227 mph
Maximum	64,410 kg		Take-off distance	1,290 m
Maximum weapon cargo	9,071 kg		Operational range	1,496 miles plus 3 hours in zone

The observation windows for watching the surface, and several navigation instruments including satellite controlled positioners and complex communication equipment.

Fighter

All these elements aid in locating a target, which can then be attacked using a varied range of arms, either stored in the internal bay (3.91 m long, 2.03 m wide and 0.88 m deep) or on the under-wing supports. Submarines are usually fought with depth charges or up to four Mk-46 model 5 or 324 mm Mk-50 light torpedoes with homing devices. These explode on contact either on or near the target. Surface vessels can be attacked with 70 mm rockets, free-falling bombs or AGM-84 "Harpoon" anti-surface missiles with homing devices once given an approximate reference point for targeting in a radius of 60 miles.

FIGHTER

The US Marines dedicated a lot of time and effort to the observation of Soviet submarine maneuvers so that, should conflict arise, they would immediately know where to send planes, submarines and warships to take them out.

Often added are the multi-purpose short range AGM-65D "Maverik" missiles with interior destructive power and the homing air-to-air "Sidewinder" missiles, which give them a certain amount of self-defence.

They can also use mines, and transport six 907 kg mines under the wings and another three in the bay, or launch Mk-57 nuclear bombs with 5 or 10 kiloton warheads, which on exploding under the water create a force that is strong enough to break the shell of a submarine.

CAMOFLAGE
The new blue-grey camouflage of the Spanish Orions makes them visually harder to detect because of the similarity in colour to that of both the sea and the sky.

SEARCH
Night searches for ships and wrecks are assisted by the powerful searchlight supported beneath the wings, and are backed up by other electronic equipment.

DETECTOR
The P-3's tail is fitted with a magnetic abnormality detection mechanism, used in the detection of submarines by comparing the magnetism of a given area with that of another.

ncreasing the area in which any type of airplane or helicopter can operate obviously makes any kind of exploratory, transport or combat mission more effective. Therefore, airplanes have been created or adapted to receive fuel whil in the air.

Such methods are now a basic element of any air force and are used in all military conflicts. The only limitation to the amount of time a plane can stay in the air is the endurance of the actual pilot who controls it.

REFUELING

The KC-10 is the biggest refuelling plane in service; the fuel it carries can be supplied to fleets of fighters, bombers and transport planes, enormously contributing to the United States Air Force's capabilities.

Origins

The first mid-air fueling operations took place as long ago as 1923 on the DH-4, and since then huge developments have followed. So huge, in fact, that a fleet of fighter or bomber planes can now take-off in one continent, carry out an attack in another, and return back to the same base without ever needing to land.

Need

Air missions that have needed the support of mid-air fueling include the bombing by Israeli F-16s of an Iraqi nuclear center

MULTINATIONAL

An American refueller KC-135 supplies a French Mirage F-1, whil a German Tornado waits its turn to do the same.

near Osirak. The annual training deployments of Spanish F-18 "Hornet" fighter-bombers at the air base at Nellis (Nevada), the deterrent actions of the American F-111s over Libya, and the deployments from Saudi Arabia during the conflict with Iraq.

This requirement is increasingly becoming more important for fighter and transport squadron pilots, because missions tend now to be longer and to require the transportation of more material and armaments. This extra load takes up a lot of the available space for fuel, therefore planes need the capacity to be refueled without having to repeatedly rely on support from the ground.

Concept

Mid-air refueling is basically the transfer of fuel from one plane to another; one plane supplies fuel, and the other one receives it. For this to be possible, in some cases both airplanes need to undergo a considerable amount of modernization.

The receiver must have some form of intake for the fuel, which is normally a fixed or removable tube that can be mechanically extended when needed. Although some planes use a receptacle built into the upper part of the fuselage. The supply-plane must have the capacity for an enormous quantity of fuel, although sometimes these planes draw from their own built-in or under-wing tanks.

They also need a pumping system and transfer apparatus such as the fixed probe and basket hose, and both planes need to be fitted with the necessary equipment for overseeing the operation.

Types

An increase in the sphere of influence and range, the reduction of take-off limitations and the greater chances of returning from missions are some of the advantages of the air refueling procedure, and so several techniques have been developed.

These include refueling over a point, in which the supply-plane waits by flying in circles around a given meeting point. Refueling en route, in which the supply-plane follows the receiver along a part of its

journey. Circular refueling when weather conditions are bad, and emergency refueling in which the supply-plane flies to the point, at which the airplane that requires its services is located.

The first three of these methods require the establishment of an ARCP (Air Refueling Control Point) and an ARCT (Air Refueling Control Time), and alternatives should be determined in case the first attempt proves unsuccessful. Different factors such as speed, altitude, amount of fuel and navigational routes need to be calculated before such operations can be made.

Models

Although several means have been used for refueling planes and helicopters, the

market offers a wide range of specially designed or transformed models to carry out such operations with maximum reliability.

Better

Active during the Gulf War, when 60,600 hours of flight and 26,000 refueling operations took place, the airplanes of the US Air Force Strategic Air Command include Boeing KC-135 and Douglas KC-10A, of which the fleet of 700 is the biggest in the world. The former, known as the "Strato-

tanker", is also used by France. The French have recently acquired three more examples of this plane, the only one specifically designed for air refueling operations. Since 1954, 732 units have been produced, six hundred of which are being restructured and supplied with General Electric/SNECMA CFM56 jet engines. This increases the original fuel cargo capacity of 68,500 liters by 50%. The new plane is called KC-135R.

Meanwhile, the "Extender", as the latter is known, has developed from the DC-10 civilian airplane. 60 units had been built by 1989, capable of carrying 197,289 liters and equipped with both a fixed probe and under-wing container system, allowing it to perform two different types of air refueling.

Varied

Other countries use a wide variety of different planes, such as the Super Etendard attacker planes that the French use. They are equipped with a shifting container, usually the "Sargent Fletcher", as part of transformations based on the civilian transport Boeing 707 airplanes. These are available at reduced prices since their withdrawal from service from several airlines.

For carrying out this task, the British aviation industry has configured models such as the British Aerospace VC10 K.Mk3, which entered service in 1983, it has the capacity for 123,000 liters and the Lockheed L-1011-500 "Trustier", which entered service in 1986 and can carry 210,000 liters on strategic missions such as cargo

transport. In Russia, there are models such as the Ilyushin II "Midas" with supply containers under the wings and the Tupolev Tu-16N.

Adaptations of the original Boeing 707 airframe are widely used in countries like Spain, Australia, Brazil, Canada, Iran, Israel and Morocco. They have been fitted with supply tanks in the fuselage and containers under the wings for air refuelling operations. Some of them were simultaneously modified for such tasks as transportation and electronic surveillance. They are outstanding for their multiple uses, and can quickly be transformed from regular transport aeroplanes into air refuellers. The "Hercules" type KC-130 is used in ten

> **DUTCH**
>
> Made from several DC-10 civilian aircraft, these Dutch KDC-10s include a telerobotic refueling system that uses television cameras and advanced technological systems to refuel the F-16 fighter planes that fly alongside it.

countries, among which are the five used by Squadron 312 of Wing 31 at Zaragoza in Spain.

Conversions

"Sargent Fletcher" type containers can be attached to practically any kind of aircraft in order to support fleets with an air refueling service. They are of a manageable, lightweight size, and are used in planes like the Grumman KA-6D of the US Marines, being positioned on under-wing supports designed to hold the auxiliary fuel tanks so as to allow the connection of the tanks on the wings and the fuselage with the exterior ones.

For this purpose there is a small built-in

TECHNICAL CHARACTERISTICS

	KC-130	KC-135	KC-10
COST IN MILLIONS OF DOLLARS	31,5	40	60
DIMENSIONS:			
Length in meters	29.79	41.4	55.2
Height in meters	11.66	11.6	17.7
Wingspan in meters	40.41	39.9	50.3
WEIGHT:			
Empty in kilograms	34,686	44,464	108,975

Maximum in kilograms	79,380	160,000	268,000
Maximum fuel load			
in litres	45,000	100,000	197,289
PROPULSION	18,032 hp	32,000 kg	71,400 kg
FEATURES:			
Maximum altitude in meters	8,075	15,240	12,800
Maximum speed in mph	361	564	578
Take-off distance in meters	1,091	1,200	1,200
Operative range in miles	1,200	1,110	2,124

CONTAINER

A refueling container usually contains an external mechanism that connects to the receiving plane, a long hose that leaves a certain leeway of movement and a pumping device built into the container itself.

ver aircraft, which can be transporters, fighters or even helicopters. Using more than one of these planes, but assigning them to different tasks, can be particularly useful. That way, some can carry armaments, and others can supply the planes with the necessary fuel to increase their operative range.

engine at the front that is connected to an air-powered turbine that pumps the fuel. A digital control unit, the corresponding opening and closing valves and an electrically powered winch that rolls and unrolls a long hose-pipe whose valve connects to the fixed or removable tube of the other plane. This makes it easier to approach recei-

SIMPLICITY

Modern refueling equipment makes the transfer process a quick and simple operation, thus reducing the chances of either plane being spotted and subsequently attacked by the enemy.

U sed for pilot training and in light tactical support missions by the air forces of Spain, Jordan, Honduras and Chile, the "Aviojet" is a second generation basic training jet and has some interesting characteristics and its features are adjusted to the inexpensive cost of buying and maintaining the vehicle.

They were ready between October 1979 and the end of 1982. Becoming squadron 793 of the General Air Academy (AGA) at San Javier in Murcia, and are now used by pilot trainers in the acrobatic patrol group "Águila".

In 1980, a further 28 units were ordered by Group 41 at Zaragoza for training pilots that were not specialized in flying jet planes. These received the Spanish Air Force codename E.25 "Mirlo". Group 41 has since moved to the Matacán group of schools at Salamanca. That same year, Chile ordered its first unit, which it received in 1981, starting off a healthy sales relationship between the two countries, with a total of fourteen BBs and thirteen CC "Halcón" being constructed with the partial support of the ENAER company.

A version with slightly different avionics was ordered later by Honduras, and in 1987 and 1988, Jordan received its order of sixteen CCs. In the 1990s, the F-5 was removed from tactical support activity, obliging the EA to use C-101s as an alternative for Wing 21 at Morón, and it was also used as a support plane on secondary missions.

Project

Deep in crisis after the cancellation of the C-401 transporter, the Spanish company Construcciones Aeronáuticas, SA (CASA) founded a new project in 1974 to design a jet engine plane for basic and advanced pilot training in the 1980s and 90s. The proposal was accepted by the Ministerio del Aire on 10th January 1975.

Sales

After a remarkably short development program, thanks to the support of the German MBB and the American company Northrop, the EC-ZDZ prototype was launched on 27th May 1977 and made its first flight a month later. In 1978, after detailed evaluations of the four prototypes, the Spanish Air Force (Ejército del Aire–EA) made an order for 60 units of type EB.

Dimensions

Much of the success of Aviojet C-101 is owed to its extraordinarily cheap cost-little more than 7 million per unit. Neither is it particularly large measuring 12.5 meters in length and little more than four meters high. When Fully loaded it weighs 6,300 kilograms, and the maximum external cargo that it can carry is 2,250 kilograms. This may include weapons that can destroy lightly defended secondary objectives.

Options

The opportunity to use this plane on complementary ground support missions, was the inspiration for work on a version with a more powerful engine and modified equipment, which was called the BB series

---

EFFECTIVE

The C-101 effectively combines simplicity and strength; meaning that the users of this basic training aircraft are generally very satisfied with a cheap and easily-managed product.

MULTI-ROLE

Despite lacking the power for certain missions, the C-101 has proved its ability for successfully completing its missions, and Wing 21 also use it as a tactical support plane.

---

and was bought by Chile and Honduras. With even greater improvements was the CC version, with a wider range of features and specialized systems such as General Instrument AN/AKLR/66 radar warning, and HUD GEC Ferranti FD 4513 head up display, CASA SCAR-81 weapons control, better telecommunications, an Avimo RGS2 weapon targeting sight and the possibility of carrying up to 2,250 kilograms of bombs, rockets and missiles. The fuselage is able to have a 30 mm cannon, or two 12.70 x 99 mm machine guns, fitted to it. Meanwhile, three supports for 250, 375 and 500-kg loads can be connected to each wing, and the low consumption renders auxiliary fuel tanks unnecessary.

The alternative of using it as a fighter

that permit it to pass from +7.7 to -3.99 Gs.

Configuration

The student sits in the front seat and the instructor behind, both in Martin-Baker Mk10 ejector seats, enjoying excellent visibility due to the high cockpit and the canopy design. Support is offered by a respiratory system using oxygen stored in high-pressure bottles, and an advanced air and pressure conditioning system designed by Hamilton Standard. The instruments include analogue and digital mechanisms to maximize the opportunitys for the student to try out the many and varied flight control systems. From both positions the hydraulic action surface control can be hand-operated.

Power

Three tanks built into each wing and another flexible one in the fuselage give a total capacity for 2,414 liters of JP-4 fuel, 2,337 liters of which can be supplied from the same point at 1,670 liters a minute. This high fuel capacity, coupled with the low consumption of the only Garrett TFE-731-2-2J jet engine, which produces 1,678 kg of thrust, makes it highly autonomous and it can perform two training missions in one hour and ten minutes without needing refueling. It only uses some 550 pounds an hour at cruise speed at 30,000 feet.

plane, and the high marketing potential of such a configuration, led to the creation of an even more powerful variant, the DD, whose prototype flew for the first time on 20th May 1985. Equipped with jet engines that offer 2,132 kilograms of thrust and a built-in navigation and attack system, this model was adequate not only for flight technique and weapons management training prior to using specialized combat aircraft, but also for supporting more powerful planes on genuine missions.

For this, it has inertial and mission computers and control and display units, linked by a 1553 database for carrying out air-to-air and air-to-land surface. It is also able to fly low by using HOTAS (Hands on Throttle and Stick) controls, which make this plane a highly efficient weapon user. This is shown by the plane's ability to perform such attack modes as Continued Calculation of Impact Point (CCIP), Continued Tracking (CT) and Continued Calculation of Impact Line (CCIL).

Trainer

To serve the plane's principal function as an economic and capable training vehicle, a modular fuselage was built, simplifying the manufacturing process it is highly resistant to withstand the hard conditions of training and attack missions. It has an estimated life span of 10,000 hours and limiting factors

ACROBATIC

The Spanish "Águila" patrol group is made up of teachers from the Academia General del Aire at San Javier. They use the "Aviojet" for their air displays all over the world. These planes are painted more colorfully so that the spectators can see them more clearly, and give off spectacular colored smoke patterns.

HALCÓN

Assembled by the Chilean company ENEAR, the Halcon are used both in training and for light attacks, and therefore have more powerful engines and a greater capacity for holding more sophisticated weaponry on the wing supports.

So, this is a very quiet plane, that is cheap to run, has a low infra-red signature, and incorporates a processor that monitors its performance and checks that its working parameters are not exceeded.

Although many users have demanded an increase of power for certain tasks, the engine can still move the airplane enough to take-off in thirteen seconds over a distance of 560 meters. The flaps are folded

on reaching a speed of 190 knots and the undercarriage is retracted at 200.

ATTACK

On the under-wing supports more than two tons of weapons can be stored that can destroy lightly defended secondary objectives and are also used for limited risk armed patrol.

MISSIONS

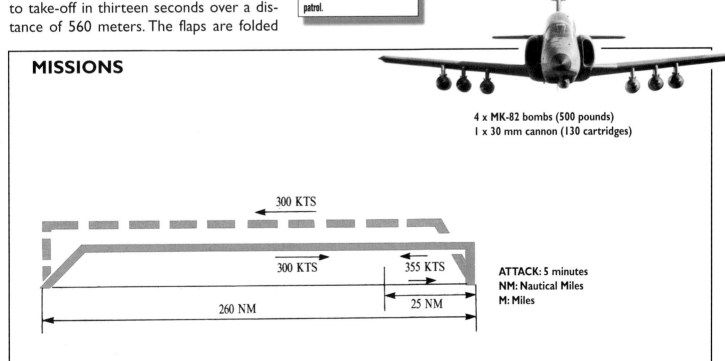

4 x MK-82 bombs (500 pounds)
I x 30 mm cannon (130 cartridges)

300 KTS

300 KTS   355 KTS

260 NM   25 NM

ATTACK: 5 minutes
NM: Nautical Miles
M: Miles

MANOUVERABILITY

Moved by a conventional transmission mechanism and supported by electric servoengines, the tail controls are highly effective and maximize the required maneuverability of training missions.

PROPULSION

"Aviojet" has an easily maintained low-consumption Garrett TFE-731 turbofan engine, which produces thrust between 1,678 kg on early versions to the 2,132 kg of the DD.

WING

The one-piece NORCASA-15 wing gives "Aviojet" excellent aerodynamics and a rigid structure. These qualities improve the maneuvering parameters it can reach.

ROBUST

The main undercarriage is strong enough to put up with the rough treatment of students getting used to the jet engines. The aerodynamic central brake is just in front of it.

INTAKES

On both sides of the cockpit are the air intakes. The air that enters here helps improve the engine performance without interfering with the forward movement of the plane.

INSTRUMENTS

The instruments in the most basic version of "Aviojet" include all that the student needs to get used to the controls of simple jet aircraft. They are easy to understand and use.

TANDEM

Sat on their Martin-Baker Mk10 ejector seats, the pilot and instructor travel in an environment specifically designed for instruction, and the canopies are designed to permit all-round vision.

POINTED

Replacing the more rounded original design, C-101s have a pointed nose to improve the aerodynamics. It covers a bay inside that contains auxiliary equipment and systems. Underneath are the wheels of the undercarriage.

TECHNICAL CHARACTERISTICS: C-101DD

COST:	7 million dollars	Internal fuel	2.414 kg
DIMENSIONS:		**PROPULSION:**	
Length	12.50 m	One Garrett TFE-731-5 jet engine giving 2,132 kg thrust	
Height	4.25 m	**FEATURES:**	
Wingspan	10.60 m	Maximum altitude	13,410 m
Wing surface	20 m²	Maximum speed	0,8 Mach
Flap surface	2.5 m²	Take-off distance	560 m
WEIGHT:		Combat range	360 miles with a 30 mm canon and two "Maverick" missiles
Empty	3,470 kg		
Maximum	6,300 kg	Maximum range	2,224 miles
Maximum external cargo	2,250 kg	Design charge factor	+7.5 Gs

The need for co-operation between European defence industries led the French and Germans to produce an advanced training airplane for preparing the pilots against a possible invasion from the Eastern bloc of Europe.

Called "Alpha Jet", this model was the first of a family of training jets with the secondary capability of ground attack. Later models such as the Argentinean IA-63 "Pampa" and the Polish PZL "Mielec" I-22 included several features of the "Alpha Jet".

Trainer

At the 1969 Le Bourget show, scale models of the P-375 were presented, made by the German Dornier company, and the Br-126, made by the French Dassault-Breget. After studying both propositions, and also the Eurotrainer E-650 made by Nord and MBB, the French and German governments decided, on 23rd July 1970, to go ahead with "Alpha Jet", a combination of the first two companies' efforts.

Development

Although the German Luftwaffe said at the time that they had no need of a training aircraft, and that they were more interested in a light attack aircraft, work continued on a multi-role craft that could serve both roles. On 16th February 1972 the intentions of the two corresponding air forces to produce two hundred units was announced. Three months ahead of the contracted schedule, the first of four prototypes flew on 26th October 1973. One

SCHOOL

314 Training Group at the base in Tours owns most of the French "Alpha Jet" fleet, used, as in other countries, for pilot training.

month later Belgium announced their desire to purchase 33 models.

In March 1975 production was authorised, and reached a rate of 13 models a month at the three production plants. Those destined for Germany were completed by 1982, and those headed for France by 1985. At their Oberpfaffenhoffen plant the German company Dornier worked on wing assembly, the tail, horizontal stabilisers, the rear end of the fuselage and the undercarriage doors. SABCA in Belgium manufactured the flaps and fuselage nose.

The French Dassault-Breguet, now Dassault Aviation, worked on the cockpit area and the manufacture and assembly of the central fuselage. The final assembly took place in all three countries.

Projects

Out of the original design, several task-specific adaptations have been developed. Among these are the MS2 with a navigation and attack system that has allowed it to participate on support missions in Egypt and Cameroon. More advanced are the "Alpha Jet" 2 NGEA (Nouvelle Génération pour Ecole e Appui) with a SAGEM navigation and attack system that launches, among others, "Magic" air-to-air missiles and AIM-39 "Exocet" anti-surface missiles, and has improved Larzac O4-C20 engines for transporting heavier loads. The prototype for "Alpha Jet" 3 included multifunction display screens, an infrared search system, electronic counter-measuring and other improvements.

«PATRUOUILLE DE FRANCE»
Used here by the French "Armee de l'Aire" in one of their famous air displays, spectators get to see the advanced qualities of the "Alpha Jet".

TRAINER
Designed as an advanced, powerful training jet, the "Apha Jet" has developed into differing variants that include advanced cabin displays, providing the practice necessary before pilots move onto the modern fighter-bombers that are appearing on the market.

The current market includes a variation that includes ATS (Air Training System) on the fighter-bomber "Rafale". This incorporates a human-machine flight cockpit that aids performance as much in training as on support missions.

Users

The initial production target was for 200 models per air force involved in the project, and over five hundred have already been completed. They are used in Belgium, where they have 33 of them, Cameroon, Egypt, that bought 45 (assembling 37 of them themselves at the local AOI industry). France, that uses 107 of their 175 models for the "Patrouille de France" air displays, Ivory Coast, Morocco, that uses their 24 models for ground attacks. Nigeria, Qatar, Togo and Germany, that still use 35 of their 175 aircraft, and have given some forty aircraft to Portugal in return for the use of their air space for training missions.

Dimensions

"Alpha Jet" weighs 3,515 kilograms, but can carry loads heavier than it's own weight, taking it up to 8,000 kiligrams. It is 13.23 meters long and 4.18 meters high-by no means the largest plane of its class, but neither is it exorbitantly expensive. The production cost of 12 million dollars puts this vehicle within the price range of any adequately-funded air force, as is suggested by some of the countries that have opted for this model.

Features

The initial need to share training work with full combat has caused the design to incorporate some features that one would not normally see in such aircraft.

Propulsion

Two double shaft Larzac 04-C6 jet engines, with a computerized hydro-mechanic control system, provide a total thrust of 2,700 kilograms, which allow the plane to carry out its expected tasks without problems. In tests it has reached speeds over 0.95 Mach. The two-engine formula was designed and constructed by

COOPERATION

The result of a co-operative program between French and German aeronautic companies, the "Alpha Jet" has been a huge market success, with 500 units produced that have spent more than a million hours in the air.

IMPROVED

Updated for ground attack operations, the "Alpha Jet" 2 incorporates more powerful engines, an integrated weapons system and complementary equipment such as a telemetric laser and a frontal presenter. Egypt and Canada have purchased this version.

Turbomeca and SNECMA, in collaboration with Klöcker-Humbolt-Heutz, Motoren Turbo Union and Fabrique Nationale. The formula provides additional security and also means that, while one engine runs normally, the other can be used to practice turning engines on and off in mid-flight.

A very low double air intake is located on either side of the fuselage, with a de-icing system and the ability to take in to 28 kilograms of air a second. These features allow the plane to travel upwards at 3,360 meters a minute, one of the fastest planes of its class.

Advantages

Its enormous operational flexibility means it can be used at every stage of a combat pilot's training, and can also participate on genuine combat missions without the need of any kind of modification. Among the most significant characteristics are the tandem seating positions with a transparent canopy that provides excellent visibility, flight controls that ensure safe and simple piloting, a resistant undercarriage that can land on unprepared surfaces and highly efficient brakes.

The plane also stands out for an exceptional resistance to wind, very complete IFR instruments, an excellent operational capa-

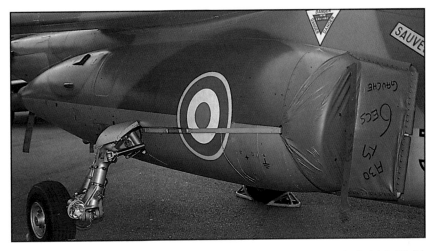

TWO-ENGINED

Set into the sides of the fuselage are the two small SNEC-MA/Turbomeca "Larzac" 04-C6 turbofan engines, which incorporate the well that the wheels fold up into.

EXHIBITION

The "Patrouille de France" flies the "Alpha Jet" in the overseas shows that promote the production capabilities of the French aeronautics industry.

---

one pilot flies on a Stencel S-III-S3AJ zero-zero ejector seat, from which the pilot can be ejected from any altitude. A HUD Kaiser/VDO KM808 overhead sight, an Elettronica ELT/156 radar warning receptor, a Lear Sieger LSI 6000E flight path and altitude reference system and a Doppler Lieft LDN inertial navigator, are important features on attack missions that might include the destruction of helicopters and the pursuit of transport and observation aircraft.

The French models, on the other hand, use a Martin-Baker ejector seat, and are equipped with gyro-directional TACAN AN/ARN-52, THOMSON CSF-902 sights and VOR/ILS approach equipment.

city that includes refueling in five minutes, an integrated ignition and cockpit access system and a ten liter tank, situated at the front, that provides liquid oxygen for a whole day's training.

Equipment

The German models, identifiable for their more pointed noses, have more advanced avionics for carrying out support actions in which, to reduce weight, only

Performances

Apart from its basic function as an advanced training aircraft, other versions are targeted at other functions. In Germany it is equipped with a 27 mm Mauser gun in a central mounting for short-range support missions, and provided with sup-

TECHNICAL CHARACTERISTICS

COST:	12 million dollars	Internal fuel	2.030 kg
DIMENSIONS:		**PROPULSION:**	
Length	13.23 m	Two SNECMA/Turbomeca "Larzac" 04-C6 non-post-combustion jet	
Height	4.19 m	engines providing 1,350 kg of pressure	
Wingspan	9.11 m	**FEATURES:**	
Wing surface	17.50 m²	Maximum altitude	14,630 m
WEIGHT:		Maximum speed	550 mph
Empty	3,515 kg	Take-off distance	370 m
Maximum	8,000 kg	Maximum range	2.400 miles
Maximum external cargo	2,500 kg	Maximum design charge factor	+12/-6.4

ports on each wing for cluster and free-fall bombs, or additional fuel tanks. Another variant is equipped with battlefield surveillance sensors.

Other proposals include training with bombs and rockets, which is done by two French squadrons that include a central mounting for a 30 mm rapid-fire DEFA gun

COCKPIT
The two-seat cockpit has excellent visibility for both the student and instructor, and has been specially designed for the tasks required of the airplane.

on their planes. The Egyptians have different attack configurations that rely on the ability of the planes to carry up to 2,500 kilograms of weapons. An anti-surface configuration includes an Aeroespatiale "Exocet" missile and a 310-liter fuel tank which balances the missile during the flight and is discarded after the missile has been launched.

UPDATED COCKPIT
The front and sections of the cockpit "Alpha Jet" ATS have updated display systems that maximize the plane's potential in training and the simple combat missions assigned to it (left photograph).

ATTACK
The basic missions of the German "Alpha Jet" involve attacking lightly protected ground targets, for which the plane is supplied with a wide range of free-fall and guided weapons (right photograph).

Designed to satisfy the training needs of the Italian Air Force, the Aermacchi MB-339 is a light jet trainer, easily mano-euvrable and cheap to maintain, and it can also be used for support and auxiliary missions.

Conception

The training plane MB-339 has sold very well, and in the early 1970s more than eight hundred were sold to the air forces of Argentina, Australia, Brazil, Dubai, Ghana, Italy, Paraguay, South Africa, Togo, Tunisia, Zaire and Zambia. This inspired the Italian company Aermacchi to work on a two-seater to satisfy more complex requirements.

Requirements
To satisfy the plan to create an aircraft

SUCCESS
An evolution of the widely used MB-326, the MB-339 has attained notable success with two hundred sales to countries that have found the Italian training plane to be capable of carrying out training tasks and also joining in on other missions.

CAPABLE
The ability to transport and use different weapon systems gives the plane additional options as a combat aircraft, serving on support, scouting and exploratory missions.

ACROBATIC
The Italian "Frecce Tricolori" patrol uses the MB-339 in their famous air displays, although two once collided and came down over the spectators.

for use in basic and intermediate training, which would reduce the number of models needed in a fleet, a program was scheduled for the flight trials of a new prototype, beginning on 12th August 1976.

Called MB-339 and identified as MM588 the results led to the production order of 100 units for the AMI (Aeronática Militare Italiana), the first of which were handed over from 8th August 1979 as MB-339A. They were also assigned to calibration assistance tasks at the Base de Pratica di Mare and to the "Frecce Tricolori" air dis-

play patrol, who received a version called PAN without side tanks or external underwing supports.

Service
The use by the Italians and the continued exhibiting of its possibilities by the "Frecce Tricolori" was excellent promotion for an airplane that caught the atten-

tion of Peru and Tunisia. Though less than expected, orders arrived from the Argentinean Marina, receiving 10 units in 1980 in time for surveillance and light attack during the Falklands Conflict. The Peruvian Air Force received 16 units between 1981 and 1982, the Malaysian air Force acquired 12 between 1983 and 1984, Dubai obtained 2 in 1984 and 3 in 1987, Nigeria obtained 12 in 1985 and Ghana bought 2 in 1987.

MB-339
Designed to fulfil the requirements of its time, the MB-339 has been updated to make up what is now the Italian training fleet.

pit complied with, between 1991 and 1993, the New Zealand Royal Air Force's order for 12. A further six were ordered by Eritrea, which they began receiving in 1997. Italy itself received the 15 CDs in 1998 as back up for their older models. All this

Dimensions

The Italian Air Force had requested a cheap jet trainer, although the Aermacci costs about 55.7 million dollars, which is hardly economical for an aircraft of this type. The plane measures 11.24 meters long and less than four meters in height, with a wingspan of 11.22. The MB-339FD weighs 6,350 kg when fully-loaded it does not carry an enormous cargo, but more than sufficient for the kind of tasks that are required of this light vehicle. In fact, although it was only planned for use in training it has actually been employed on genuine surface attack missions.

Implementation

The sales of the basic models and the manufacture of a new range with secondary ground attack capabilities for Italy were crowned by the presentation of Veltro II, a one-seater version for use in light attack. A more advanced model called MB-339C first flew in 1985. Its better features, more powerful engines and modern cock-

makes a total production of over two hundred units to date.

Export

Some failed contracts, such as that of the JPATS for the US Marines and Air Force which went to Lockheed, pushed Italian designers to update their model into a new variant, planned for export, called FD.

This model includes all the latest avionics technology. The cockpit is ultra-modern, with multi-purpose display screens and an air-refueling probe, operational elements that pilots need to be familiar with before they can move on to pilot more advanced aircraft.

Digital

Created for training pilots to use the latest fighter planes, the MB-339FD "Full

Digital" maintains the basic design but introduces many improvements for carrying out its training missions and light attacks. The cockpit configuration is very advanced in comparison with other contemporary designs.

Avionics

The two pilots are seated in tandem as in the earlier designs in Martin-Baker MK10LK ejector seats that guarantee escape at any altitude, and enjoy the same excellent visibility of the previous versions.

A built-in avionics system, connected by a databus with fiber-optic cables to reduce failure, has been incorporated to satisfy future requirements. Also worthy of mention are the three multi-functional color display screens, of differing and interchangeable formats depending on the pilot or instructor's particular needs for a given mission. A HUD sight provides all the data one would need on a training flight; weapons are operated by a HOTAS system with a single multiple activation control. Complex navigation equipment include an inertial laser platform and a complete self-defence system with transmission detec-

TECHNICAL CHARACTERISTICS MB-339FD

COST:	55.7 million dollars		Internal fuel	1,871 l
DIMENSIONS:			**PROPULSION:**	
Length	11.24 m		One Rolls-Royce Viper MK680-43 jet engine providing	
Height	3.9 m		1,996 kg of pressure	
Wingspan	11.22 m		**FEATURES:**	
Wing surface	19.3 m²		Maximum altitude	14,020 m
Flap surface	2.21 m²		Maximum speed	552 mph
WEIGHT:			Speed with containers	589 mph
Empty	3,414 kg		Take-off distance	550 m
Maximum	6,350 kg		Maximum range	1,229 miles
Maximum external cargo	1,815 kg		Design charge factor	+7.33/-4 Gs

tors, decoy flare launchers and the possibility of connecting electronic combat equipment onto the under-wing supports.

Airframes

Keeping the earlier configuration, which has proved to be simple, functional and easily to mantain, the airframe has been updated after 350.000 hours of flight in differing weather conditions, and can withstand 24,000 landings and 10,000 hours of flight indicating that the plane has a long life span.

Configured with new materials that resulted from investigations into operations in cold conditions. The airframe is now more resistant and easier to repair than its predecessors. The plane has been designed to have highly accessible systems and equipment, thus simplifying maintenan-

TWO-SEATER

The cockpit of the MB-339 incorporates all those basic elements needed for advanced training and has been updated with all the latest display technology.

ATTACK

The ability to transport all kinds of weapons, electronic warfare containers and fuel tanks increase the CD version's capabilities both in combat and in use in all phases of advanced pilot training.

ce related tasks. At the same time, the integrated flight control systems include conventional control surfaces alongside elec-

tronically activated ones, reducing vulnerability at low altitude.

Power

Reliable and with low consumtion, the Rolls-Royce 640 jet engine is the result of a long development process using new technology, making the plane much safer.

The engine's simple design, sturdiness, low number of components and low operational temperature, increase its life span and chances of passing the inspections it receives every 1,200 hours. Its consumption is not unlike that of other jet engines. It generates a thrust of 1,996 kilograms and the fuel tanks on the fuselage and built into the wings can be filled at high pressure from the same intake. If necessary, two tanks can be installed at the center of the wings or use can be made of the air refuelling probe, which is really provided with

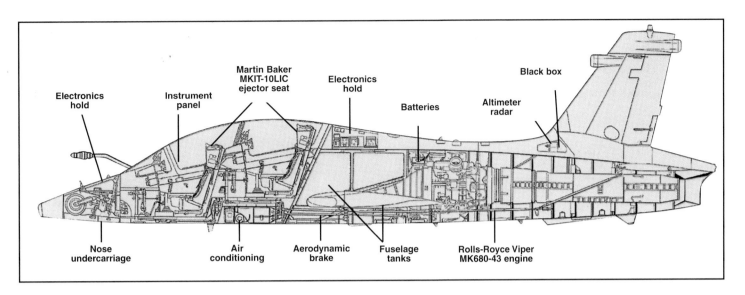

Electronics hold · Instrument panel · Martin Baker MKIT-10LIC ejector seat · Electronics hold · Batteries · Altimeter radar · Black box

Nose undercarriage · Air conditioning · Aerodynamic brake · Fuselage tanks · Rolls-Royce Viper MK680-43 engine

training flights in mind, but would also be very useful in increasing autonomy on naval patrol missions in search of surface objectives.

Capacity

Nearly two tons of armaments can be fixed to the wing attachments. The storage system, integrated into the avionics, enables the pilot to observe and manage the load. These include two mounts for 30 millimeter DEFA guns with 125 rounds each. Up to 250 kg of free-fall bombs, BAT-120 tactical bombs and BAT-100s. 59, 68 and 81 mm and 2.75" rocket launchers in

configurations of four or nine. Two "Maverik" air-surface missiles, two light anti-ship Marte MK-2A missiles, various anti-submarine scatter rockets, containers for electronic warfare equipment or for the transport of personal equipment, and smoke generators for air shows. Two auxiliary fuel tanks with capacity for 330 liters and two Matra "magic" or AIM-9 "Sidewinder" infrared air-to-air missiles, which work together with other air-to-air or air-to-surface missiles, giving the student a wide range of functions to practice and allowing the plane to serve on additional low-risk missions.

MARTE MK2 A

C hosen by 17 users all over the world, who have bought more than 750 units. The British Aerospace "Hawk" is a highly manageable training aircraft, as much designed for training purposes as for light attacks. It has over a million hours of flight use behind it since first entering service in the British RAF (Royal Air Force).

Training

To comply with the British military staff's specifications for an advanced training aircraft for teaching flying and weapon-using operations, on 1st October 1971 the HS1182 project was chosen. After ordering the production of 176 units in March 1972, the first five of which were used in different trials, the first completed unit was marketed in 1974 and in November 1976 the RAF began handing over those units destined for the base at R.A.F.

«GOSHAWK»
Produced by McDonnell Douglas under the name of T-45A, this plane is used in the basic instruction of the US Marines, and is currently being updated to include new avionics with digital displays.

Valley. Not long after, this airplane was chosen by the air display group "The Red Arrows".

ACQUISITIONS

COUNTRY	MODEL
Abu Dhabi	16 Mk63-Mk63A and 18 Mk102
Dubai	9 Mk61
Finland	50 Mk51 and 7 Mk51A
Indonesia	20 Mk53, 8 Mk100 and 16Mk200
Kenya	12 Mk52
South Korea	20 Mk67
Kuwait	12 Mk64 1of which 5 remain
Malaysia	10 Mk108 and 18 Mk208
Oman	4 Mk103 and 12 Mk203
Saudi Arabia	30 Mk65
Switzerland	20 Mk66
United Kingdom	176 Mk-1 of which 100 are still in service[a]
US Navy	187 T-45[a]
Zimbabwe	8 Mk60 and 6 Mk60A
Canada - NATO School	25 Mk100
British Aerospace	2 Mk60/102 and 3 Mk200
Australia	33 Mk100

Attack

Purchased by Abu Dhabi, South Korea, Oman, Finland, Zimbabwe, Dubai, Indonesia, Kenya, Kuwait, the USA, Saudi Arabia, Malaysia, Australia, Brunei and the Canadian school for students of NATO (the North Atlantic Treaty Organisation), among other countries, the performance, multi-role and design qualities of this airplane are indisputable.

Apart from the Mk1 version, originally used by the British for pilot training, later configurations have been the Mk-1A, the 50, 60, 100 and 200 series and the "Goshawk". The Mk-1A is the result of updating 89 units between 1983 and 1986 for short range defence missions with the installa-

> **AIR DEFENSE**
>
> Some of the British "Hawks" have been updated for participation in air defence, for which they have been equipped with under-wing supports for "Sidewinder" or "Magic" guided infrared missiles.

> **CAPABLE**
>
> The "Hawk" 100 has been equipped to introduce pilots to advanced avionics systems and the management of a wide range of weapons and electronic equipment.

tion of supports for "Sidewinder" infrared air-to-air missiles that can work together with the ADV "Tornado" missiles, although twelve of them are also used for towing air targets.

The need to comply with export orders motivated the upgrading of the 50 series to include a 30% more powerful engine and a greater range. Its cockpit is more modern and has the additional capacity for 2,060 kilograms of weapons on the under-wing supports. Another model received a more aerodynamic nose, modified flaps, new fuel tanks, better acceleration and the capacity for up to three tons of weapons. Later versions of this model included the Mk60, Mk63 and Mk67 of the 60 series.

Users

Aiming to configure a specially designed model for both training and surface attack tasks for one pilot, the 100 Series was designed begining in 1982 incorporating an Adour Mk871 engine providing 2,630 kilograms of thrust, a resigned cockpit with multi-purpose display screens and a HOTAS flight control system, laser illuminator and an infrared system installed in the nose, new ailerons at the rear and over the wings and a radar warning. This improved version had the capacity to carry 3,265 kg of weapons.

A multi-role plane was developed from the promising early version with only one seat, and the first unit took off on 19th May 1986. It can be used for photographic surveillance, in ground attack missions and action of the battlefield, or as Mk203, Mk205and Mk208 variants are available,

FIGHTER-BOMBER

Using the standard "Hawk" as the basis of its design, the 200 Series is a one-man plane with Westinghouse multimode radar and extensive possibilities for the transportation and launching of different air-to-air and air-to-surface weapons.

RED ARROWS

The British Air Force uses a transformed version of the "Hawk" for its highly successful air displays. The model has been painted brightly so that spectators can see it more clearly.

equipped with an internal 25-millimeter gun, a Westinghouse APG-66H radar and updated avionics. It has the capacity for 3.5 tons of bombs and missiles.

US Navy

Made by the American McDonnell Douglas, the T-45A "Goshawk" is an updated version used by the US Marines for basic training. Originally 187 units were planned for production, and in 1996, nine units were given to the Naval Air Station at Kingsville, Texas. 14 more entered service in 1997. More then 10,000 hours have been flown by this plane that uses a Rolls-Royce F405-RR-401 Adour jet engine, the American name for the British design, and work is currently being carried out on the new digital Cockpit 21, which will incorporate two monochrome display screens and will be used by NAS Meridian.

Configuration

Designed to be highly maneuverable and acrobatic, the latest versions include slight modifications to the wings to maximize their efficiency in combat.

Cockpit

Very good visibility from the cockpit results from a one-piece transparent acrylic canopy, which resists the impact of a one kilogram bird hit at 587 mph. The elevated rear seat, for the instructor, favors backward visibility. The pilots are separated by a panel, and sit in Martin-Baker Mk10LH rocket-assisted ejector seats, triggered by a

chord that is built into the canopy and that is activated milliseconds before launching.

Dually controlled and totally pressurised, the instruments vary from simple analogics in early versions to the multi-purpose display screens, very similar to those of the F-18 "Hornet", of the Mk100s acquired by Australia.

Capacity

All the different series are driven by Rolls-Royce Adour non-combustion jet engines, the newer ones being far more powerful than the earlier ones. This engine, complemented by a jet for ignition, is fed by two small air intakes on the sides of the fuselage, making this a very agile airplane that can participate in offensive missions.

The plane has a long range thanks to the tank that is built into the fuselage with capacity for 832 liters, and another on the wings for 823, and it can also be fitted with auxiliary tanks of 455, 591 or 864 liters inside the wings. Some models have air-refueling probes to increase the range even more and give pilots the opportunity to practice the related skills.

Avionics

The RAF's models include GEC Ferranto gyroscopes, a remote altitude indicator and a Honeywell RAI-44 magnetic detection unit, a Louis Newmark direction presenter, Sylvaria UHF and VHF communication systems, Tacan CAT 7000 and Cossor ILS and IFF Cossor 2720 friend-or-foe identifiers. The 100 Series includes electronic self-defence and guided air-to-surface missiles. The 200 Series includes radar, multi-purpose screens and a wide range of equipment that make the plane seem more like a light fighter than a training aircraft.

Armaments

A 30 millimeter Aden Mk4 cannon can be fitted underneath the fuselage along with 120 rounds, while there are either 2 or 4, depending on the model, attaching points under the wings. 81 or 100 mm rocket launchers can be fitted here, or 250-kg

AUSTRALIA
One of British Aerospace's latest successes has been the sale of the "Hawk" to Australia, consolidating its position as the biggest exporter of training jets in the world.

ADVANCED AVIONICS
Modeled on more advanced fighter-bombers, the BA "Hawk" has updated avionics in its cockpit to offer the most advanced configurations.

free-fall bombs and cluster bombs. CBLS containers hold bombs for training purposes. Other options include infrared air-to-air missiles and "Maverik" air-surface missiles, along with surveillance equipment and a Vinten camera.

DETAILS

With a modified tail increases the plane's level of performance, the "Hawk" is renowned for its wide capabilities that can include radar warning.

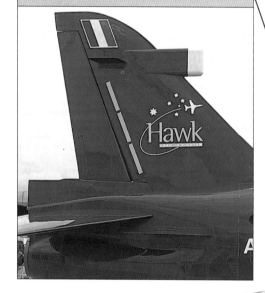

COCKPIT

Equipped with Martin-Baker ejector seats, the two-seater cockpit has a place for both the student and instructor, although when used for tactical purposes only one person occupies the plane.

UNDERCARRIAGE

The main undercarriage folds into a compartment in the fuselage after take-off. It is robust and permits landing on any kind of runway at air bases.

PROPULSION

Fed by two small, but efficient, air intakes, the "Hawk" 100 includes a Rolls-Royce Adour Mk781 turbofan engine that gives it great agility and high power thanks to the 2,630 kilograms of pressure.

WING SURFACE

The wing has been updated to satisfy the needs of air training, it is streamlined, has a strong lift and the most recent design can be equipped with infrared air-to-air missiles on external supports.

REFUELING

The inclusion of a fixed-air refueling tube allows pilots to practice this important operation, and also betters the operational range of the plane.

NOSE

The nose can be configured differently depending on the kinds of equipment installed inside, which can include light or multi-functional radar.

TECHNICAL CHARACTERISTICS HAWK 100 SERIES

COST:	19.3 million dollars	Internal fuel	1,655 l
DIMENSIONS:		External fuel	1,182 l
Length	11.68 m	**PROPULSION:**	
Height	4.16 m	One Rolls-Royce Adour Mk781 jet engine providing 2,630 kg of pressure	
Wingspan	9.34 m	**FEATURES:**	
Wing surface	16.69 m²	Maximum altitude	13,546 m
Wing surface	2.50 m²	Low flying speed	Mach 1,2
WEIGHT:		Take-off distance	640 m
Maximum	9.100 kg	Landing distance	605 m
Maximum external cargo	3.265 kg	Maximum distance	1,556 miles
		Design factor charge	+8/-4 Gs

When the Iraqi army advanced through the darkness of the night, hoping to avoid American satellites, little did they imagine that their every move was being observed by a plane specially designed for locating any kind of object moving across the earth's surface. The E-8B "Joint STARS", the name of that machine, studied the most common routes and transmitted the data concerning any land vehicles it spotted to land stations. The information served the allied forces in pin-pointing exactly where the highest concentrations of Iraqi vehicles were stationed, and subsequently attack them there.

USE

Already used by the USAF, it is expected that NATO will soon receive its own units for use in joint operations in both peacetime and conflict.

Long development

The lack of reliable methods to determining enemy movements became apparent in the Vietnam War. At that time, the only solution was to use surveillance planes, but advanced spy satellites have now become far more common.

Management

Such projects as the US Air Force's "Pave Moder" radar or the army's long range SOTAS target acquisition system were invented in the 1970s, but development was halted by the high cost. In the early 1980s, the US Army and USAF developed J-STARS, the Joint Surveillance and Target Acquisition Radar System.

Several offers were studied, stipulating that the need for the ability to detect, locate, identify, classify and follow moving hostile targets on the surface, in any climatic conditions and from a distance safe enough

ASSIGNATION

Used by the Air Combat Command of the US Air Force at Air Control Wing 93, the J-STAR lent their supportive services to the multinational campaign in Bosnia.

to avoid the threat of anti-air attacks. The Grumman Melbourne System Division's proposal was finally chosen, originally called EC-18C and later E-8A.

Development

Having decided that the equipment should be transported on a Boeing 707 type platform, which was already used as the base for the AWACS air detection system, and that it should be compatible with the Ground Station Modules (GSM) that Motorola had developed for the US Army. The contract was signed on 27th September and construction began on two 707-308Cs bought from Quantas and American Airlines.

In Wichita, Boeing revised and updated the engines and airframe, then on 31st July 1987 the first plane was unveiled at the Grumman factory in Florida. The second followed in October 1988. The adaptation of the airframe and the installation of the equipment was a relatively fast process, and the first plane took off on 22nd December 1988, and the second did likewise on 31st August the following year.

Ratification

The initial order was for 22 planes and 100 ground stations. Evaluation of the instant transmissions began at the ground stations in August 1989, and the European flight trials took place in February, March and September of 1990.

the war known as "Desert Storm" began.

The J-STARS worked a total of 535 hours in that conflict, carrying out missions of up to 14.6 hours duration. For these missions the air refueling capabilities proved useful, working alongside the pilots of F-15 fighters in eliminating Iraqi batteries of medium range "Scud" missiles.

At the same time, they identified moving and stationary Iraqi units. This information allowed them to be attacked before they could reach the frontline.

Their capabilities were shown by the destruction of 58 of the 60 tanks that comprised one advance column and in the

Midway through the ratification process, when adaptations were being made in view of those results to make provisions for all the requirements, Iraq invaded Kuwait. The two available planes were taken to the war zone, along with the technicians still working on their development, to participate in the operation to liberate Kuwait, a chance to verify the features of the planes in a real combat situation. A total of 770 tons of material, transported by a C-141 "StarLifter" and five C-5 "Galaxy" followed them to Riyadh in Saudi Arabia to arrive on the 12th January to make up Squadron 4411°.

Results

Two days later they began operating in the area, and on the morning of the 17th

images recorded of the massive Iraqi withdrawal.

Contract

The excellent results shown in combat led to a contract for the series production on 24th April 1992, this was revised in May 1993, by the addition of a further six units to those already planned. This included an E-8C ordered in November 1990.

Work

The provision for the manufacture of two per year was delayed by Boeing's withdrawal from the project, alleviated by the intervention of Northrop who continued production at their Melbourne plant. The third unit was ready in December 1993 and made its first flight on 25th March 1994, by which time three more units were ready in USAF hangers. The acquisition of three second hand planes from Canada, costing 6.8 million dollars, was also required, and these started arriving in 1996.

That same year Variant C was declared operational, of which 13 planes are destined for Wing 93 of Airborne Control and Surveillance at the Robins Air Base in Georgia.

CAPABLE

A J-STARS system can be installed in a Boeing 707, an aircraft that has proved its worth in its many years of service as a passenger airplane, and as the transporter of AWACS air detection systems.

IDENTIFICATION

Apart from the long protuberance under the fuselage, J-STARS do not differ in appearance from other Boeing 707-based designs, making them hard for the enemy to detect and subsequently destroy.

Also being considered are six units for NATO's AGS (Airborne Ground Surveillance) program, after the excellent results obtained during its support mission in the Bosnian "Joint Endeavour" operation, between 14th December 1995 and March 1996, an operation that was repeated between the end of 1996 and early 1997.

Cost and dimensions

The vehicle costs an alarming 250 million dollars to produce-one of most expensive planes of its class. It is exceptionally large-over 45 meters in length and almost twelve meters high. It is also extraordinarily heavy 77,564 kg when empty and a maximum of 152,407 kilograms

TECHNICAL CHARACTERISTICS E-8 "JOINT STARS"

COST:	250 million dollars		PROPULSION:	
DIMENSIONS:			Four Pratt & Whitney JT3D-3B jet engines providing 8,100 kg of thrust	
Length	46.61 m		**FEATURES:**	
Height	12.95 m		Maximum altitude	12,800 m
Wingspan	44.42 m		Maximum speed	Mach 0.84
WEIGHT:			Mission length	Maximum 11 hours, which go up to 20 with air refuelling
Empty	77,564 kg		Maximum range	5,400 miles
Maximum	152,407 kg		Capacity	covers six hundred square miles on an 8-hour flight
Internal fuel	87,565 l			

when fully-loaded, clearly suggesting that this aircraft can carry extremely heavy loads, and a staggering 87,565 liter load of internal fuel.

Features

Having decided on 25th September 1996 on the construction of a total of 20 units for the USAF/Army, a highly advanced program is being shared between the plant at Lake Charles, Louisiana, where the airframe is being updated and at Melbourne in Florida, where the electronics are being integrated. J-STARS can determine the direction, speed and type of activity of any surface object thanks to its Westinghouse Norden AN/APY-3 multi-mode Side-looking Phased Array radar, which operates on band I and its SAR synthetic lens electronic search system that gives it a range of 105 miles, Ceridian Data signal processors including five Raytheon Model 920/866 computers. Eighteen Interstate Electronics displays in Raytheon Model AXP-300/500 computer workstations, coded voice and data links with such equipment as JTIDS, SCDL or SINC-GARS, and other sub-systems.

The data that comes from the radar, built into a fixed structure under the fuselage, are processed on board and sent to air operators at the same time as they are transmitted to ground stations. Thanks to the high speed processors that can do 600 million operations a second, and as of 1998 include 7800 MIPS of processing capacity and 306 information-storing gigabytes.

ANTENA
The "Joint STARS" detection mechanism is produced by the Norden Corporation of Northrop Grumman, and its function is to detect, locate, classify and pursue moving and static surface targets.

Operation

The crew for standard missions is made up of 21 members, 34 on longer ones, who alternately use the six bunk beds on board. One aircraft can cover 300,000 square miles on a typical 8-hour mission at an altitude of 10,000 meters. Among its operational modes are the WAS/MTI which provides a zonal display of the battlefield, thanks to the localization and identification of targets moving in an area of 157 square miles. In each area it can differentiate between wheel or tracked vehicles, helicopters and the SMM, which, in a similar way,

concentrates on an area of 6 square miles to provide individual displays of the moving land force. The data concerning the current and predicted positions of targets is sent, via an IDM modem, to the attacking planes; SAR/FTI creates images of almost photographic quality of the terrain, including bridges, airports and parked vehicles. This data can instantly be sent to the GSM ground stations via an extendible 30-mm telescope that contains two display consoles for later analysis and application in combat maneuveres.

TERRESTRIAL

Installed in a "Hummer" jeep, the GSM ground station, via real time coded link, receives the information recorded by the airborne radar, and can be acted upon immediately.

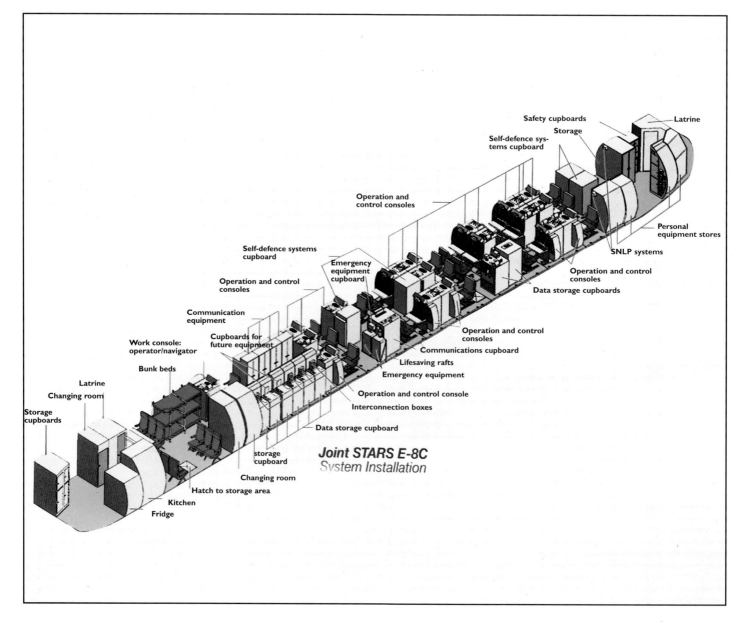

Safety cupboards

Latrine

Storage

Self-defence systems cupboard

Operation and control consoles

Personal equipment stores

SNLP systems

Operation and control consoles

Data storage cupboards

Self-defence systems cupboard

Emergency equipment cupboard

Operation and control consoles

Communication equipment

Operation and control consoles

Cupboards for future equipment

Communications cupboard

Work console: operator/navigator

Lifesaving rafts

Bunk beds

Emergency equipment

Latrine

Operation and control console

Changing room

Interconnection boxes

Storage cupboards

Data storage cupboard

storage cupboard

Joint STARS E-8C
System Installation

Changing room

Hatch to storage area

Kitchen

Fridge

Designed to counter the threat of different combat aircraft, early warning systems have proven to be an important step forward in neutralizing potential attacks, because they are so difficult to locate and have strong detection capabilities.

Used by the wealthiest countries, the different models of AEW (Airborne Early Warning) guarantee a high capacity of self-defence and reaction in a wide range of activities such as locating planes used for the smuggling of narcotics and crisis control in all corners of the globe.

The product of a necessity

Different models were already in service in the 1960s and 1970s, but it was in the 1980s that their popularity became most apparent, deriving from the need to cover for the absence of radar stations at certain fixed points.

The planes

An original variant is the Israeli "Phalcon" that incorporates six radar antennas into the structure of a Boeing 707, so that surveillance areas can be completly covered. The concept has been imitated by the Chileans with a similarly modified air-

craft. Another version that resembles the Israeli aircraft, is the Swedish S 100B "Argus" with a flat Erieye radar antenna over the Saab 340 turboprop, which is exported to Brazil.

The Soviet Union copied American design philosophy and installed a rotating mushroom-shaped radar over the structure of an Ilyushin Il-76 transport airplane, and about thirty A-50 "Mainstay" were produced. During the invasion of Kuwait, the Iraqis used a similar modification called "Adnan 1".

Other options include the C-130 "Hercules" with an AN/APS-145 system installed on a rotating radar dome on top of the plane, the P-3 "Orion" with a similar radar that is used by the American Customs Service, the Indian ASWAC set onto an HS 748 and the different designs that formulate the Australian "Wedgetail" program.

Domination

The powerful American defence industry dominates the market with two contrasting models. The first is the small E-2 "Hawkeye" that has been exported to Israel, Japan, Egypt, Singapore, Taiwan and the French Marine Nationale. The second, larger and more capable, is the AWACS (Airborne Warning And Control System) E-3 "Sentry" which is used by the air forces of the United States, United Kingdom, France, Saudi Arabia and NATO's early

NAVAL

Designed for use on American aircraft carriers, the E-2C "Hawkeye" is still undergoing several developments to optimize its potential in the field of aerial detection.

warning force. Japan has chosen the former system for use on a Boeing 767-200ER.

AWACS

Widely used in surveillance operations over the countries that used to make up the Warsaw Pact, during the Gulf War and in the continued attacks against Serbia, the AWACS E-3 "Sentry" is NATO's first line of detection and a basic element of the US Air Force.

Each unit costs around 300 million dollars, and first came onto the market in March 1977 under the title of E-3A and have since undergone several modifications that have led to the B and C series and those specially designed for Great Britain and France, called D and F respectively. Their detection capacity is provided by AN/APY-1 and 2 radar, modified by the recent Radar System Improvement Program. They are able to locate small radar targets and cruise missiles in an area satu-

patrols over a distance of 966 miles from its operational base. The more recent models have an air-refueling probe that allows the plane to continue its surveillance for up to eleven hours.

Naval

Designed to act as the ears and eyes of the marines and protect combat groups, the Northrop Gumman "Hawkeye" has been in service since 1964. The early models were called A, the current ones, that have been flying since 1971, are known as C.

Following a US Navy order, to which Japan has been added, an updating process of the models comprising Group I was started in 1994. Manufacture began on Group II at St Augustine in Florida. The first modernized unit, known as "Hawkeye" 2000 was unvailed on 29th April 1996. The first of the new aircraft was unveiled on 24th February 1997. Both include the new Lockheed Martin AN/APS-145 radar that can detect, identify and pursue up to two thousand targets at distances of up to three hundred miles, offering information about their movements, speed, height and (IFF) friend-or-foe identification.

The plane and equipment are controlled by a crew of five. The airframe has been updated for naval use including a system for operating in conjunction with aircraft carriers.

The normal work of the plane involves flying to a point some 180 miles away from the aircraft carrier to fly in a constant orbit at an altitude of 9,000 meters. From here it surveys air movements and transmits the information to the scout ships or air patrols made up of F-14 "Tomcat" combat aircraft.

rated by electronic counter-measures.

The crew consists of four members to control the plane, and 13 specialists who operate the 14 SDC display screens and two ADU auxiliary units. These receive data from an IBM CC-2 processor. Propulsion comes from four Pratt & Whitney TF33-PW-100A jet engines providing 9,450 kg of thrust each, allowing the plane to reach speeds of 500 mph. It can fly six-hour

CUSTOMS

US Customs uses their Lockheed P-3 AEW&C, to watch out for the possibility of unauthorized aircraft trying to enter the country, most often trying to bring in illegal drugs.

«HAWKEYE»

The ability of the E-2C to fold its wings is ideal for deployment from aircraft carriers because they occupy very little space and can easily be taken into the holds for maintenance work.

TECHNICAL CHARACTERISTICS E-2C GROUP II

COST:	200 million dollars
DIMENSIONS:	
Length	24.56 m
Height	5.58 m
Wingspan	17.6 m
Wing surface	65.03 m²
Flap surface	11.03 m²
Diameter of radar dome	7.32 m
WEIGHT:	
Empty	18,364 kg
Maximum	24,689 kg
Internal fuel	7,000 l

PROPULSION:	
Two Allison T56-A-427 turboprop engines providing 5,100 horsepower	
FEATURES:	
Maximum altitude	11,278 m
Maximum speed	376 mph
Cruise speed	288 mph
Take-off distance	564 m
Operational range	flight of 192 miles from base and 4 hours of surveillance
Maximum distance	512 miles

MULTIPLE TAIL

Updated to improve the stability of the plane and equipped with enormous radar on the fuselage, the tail is made up of four parts that channel the air current to improve the aerodynamics.

DYNAMIC INTAKE

Built into the central upper part of the fuselage is a dynamic air intake that is needed to cool the electronic equipment within the aircraft.

FUSELAGE

The interior of the fuselage of the "Hawkeye" includes a skid that protects the plane during landing and take-off, electronic detection mechanisms and a fuel exhaust tube.

PROPULSION

Built into the lower part of the main undercarriage, the E-2C incorporates two powerful Allison T56-A-427 turboprop engines, which produce a total of 10,200 horsepower and move four-rotor propellers.

RADAR

Taking advantage of the latest technological advances, Lockheed Martin offers the latest version of their AN/APS-145 radar that can detect, identify and pursue up to two thousand targets in a radius over three hundred miles from the position of the plane.

«HAWKEYE» 2000

The display in the cockpit and detection area have been introduced to the newest "Hawkeye" as part of a policy to chase up new markets.

FOLDED

The ability to fold the wings considerably reduces the size of the plane and uses up far less space on the decks of aircraft carriers. The folding process is automatic and can be controlled from inside the airplane.

Configuration

Each model has very different characteristics, but the configuration of most UAVs is basically very similar. A ground control station is normally set up in a protected shelter and transported by a truck, made up of the control mechanisms, display screens, operating posts, a small maintenance workshop, and several other elements depending on the particular mission.

On the same truck, a trailer or on another truck, the UAV is transported with its launch pad. It is either jet-engined or has a small engine that turns propellers, it has been designed to be equipped with instruments including day and night-time television cameras, real time data transmission equipment, exploration radar, normal photographic cameras, explosive charges, radio and guided frequency receivers, FLIR infrared searchers, video recorders, interferers of defined frequencies and infrared polarimetric sensors for detecting minefields. The exact inventory of the cargo is limited by the weight that the transporter can carry.

Function

Once positioned in the area that needs to be covered and having determined the nature of the mission, the appropriate sensor is attached to the remote-controlled vehicle. The machine is launched along a pre-determined routes and altitudes. Information is returned to base throughout the

Designed to obtain and transmit information efficiently and economically without putting pilot in danger, the UAV (Unmanned Aerial Vehicles) are small planes supplied with optical surveillance equipment and electronics. Their premary mission is to obtain images, frequencies and data about enemy troops that can be used to plan maneuveres that can put a fast and efficient end to the conflict.

> **ADVANCES**
>
> The use of advanced technology has permitted substantial variations on the original configuration of designs like this, whose fuselage can turn to permit vertical landings and take-offs

Implantation

In the early 1950s, the Teledyne Ryan 24 FIREBEE went into service. It was used for surveillance tasks over Cuba, for electronic interference and for dropping propaganda during the Vietnam War. These radio-controlled vehicles became particularly renowned after the Israelis used them during their humbling defeat of the Syrians in the valley of Bekaa.

With their efficiency shown, the systems underwent a process of development to be used in conflicts such as the Lebanon invasion of 1982, the war between Iran and Iraq in which the latter country used machines derived from civilian technology. They were used during the South African interventions in Angola, the "Desert Shield" and "Desert Storm" operations during the Gulf War and they are currently being used for surveillance work in the Balkans, mainly over Serbia.

> **STEALTH**
>
> Designed to use all the latest stealth technology, the PREDATOR has been bought by the US Air Force. It has an outstanding operational range and can be used on all kinds of surveillance missions.

flight on television screens. These machines can perform a wide variety of roles. They range from observing the movements of illegal immigrants as they attempt to enter Europe from North Africa, to precise images of air bases and missile stocks. These can be seen in either real time or when the plane returns. The analysis of the film and tapes is fundamental in the planning of later strategies.

After being checked and refilled, the machine can be prepared for another mission, but in some cases they are destroyed by enemy fire and a new model has to be employed.

Israelis

The Israeli's ample experience in combat has caused their defence industry to produce some of the most advanced systems available, this has helped with the success of their many military operations. The Malalt Division of Israel Aircraft Industries (IAI), famous for its modernization of all types of fighter-bombers, is considered the world leader in UAV's, for the amount of units constructed and because their designs have over 60,000 flying hours between them on three continents.

Controlled from an advanced Ground Control Station (GCS), which can simultaneously control several craft, the machines are moved by small but highly reliable long-range propeller engines. They include the SEARCHER, designed for operational and

HERON

The Israeli HERON includes a detection mechanism with television and infrared cameras, advanced features for a large vehicle, which has a much larger range than that of its predecessors.

TACTICAL

Mainly destined for operational and tactical military use, the SEARCHER, manufactured by IAI (Israeli Aircraft Industries), is used by the Israeli Armed Forces and in other countries.

tactical missions, the compact EYE-VIEW that can be used at night, the HERON designed for long missions at high altitudes to obtain strategic information, and the tactical HUNTER that has been adopted by the USA. The SCOUT and the HARPY are designs that can attack guided and detection radar, and the HERMES 750 is made by Silver Arrow.

Options

Following Israel's example, many countries have joined the frenetic race to develop new aircraft with stealth technology to avoid, or at least complicate, detection by the enemy offences.

The Russian company Yakolev flies the Yak-061 SHMEL, which has a range of 36 miles, can fly independently for two hours, and includes real time image transmission. Since 1997, the Russian Armed Forces have used, in conflicts such as that in Chechnya, the C variant of PCHELA-1, with a daytime television camera installed on a turning platform.

The Americans, on the other hand, work with models like the AAI SHADOW 600, which has been exported to Romania or the heavy PREDATOR that is used by the Orlando Military Intelligence Battalion in Florida, with the capacity for 60 hour's flight carrying loads of 210 kilograms, and incorporating "Stealth" technology to avoid detection. The Unmanned Naval Strike Aircraft made by Lockheed Martin includes the VATOL that can be launched from

submarines, and the Teledyne Ryan GLO-BAL HAWK that can be equipped with Hughes HISAR radar, and was designed to obtain synthetic images of land features up to 60 miles away.

European Industry

The strong European industry has reacted in time to satisfy the high demand for remote control surveillance systems for military and policing operations, the biggest market in the world at the moment.

France

The third biggest arms exporter in the world, France has started the manufacture of several models that satisfy both its own armed forces and those to whom it exports its products. Although the French Army has also acquired a Canadian CL-289

HUNTER
The HUNTER is a remote control surveillance plane that is used by the US Army and has been used on combat operations in which it has demonstrated an extraordinary efficiency in locating all kinds of objectives.

CZECH
Designed and produced by the Czech Republic in collaboration with Hungary, the JOJKA III includes a television image recording module that records onto a tape that can later be examined.

for the 7th Armed Regiment for use in Bosnia as part of the Dayton Agreement operations.

Among the products available are the FOX models made by CAC Systémes that fly independently for five hours and are transported by a Unimog 6x6 truck, and the HUSSARD II directed by a fibre optic link that is immune to interference, Matra's DRAGON that incorporates an integrated electronic interference system, the HUNTER used by the French Air Force, the C22 DROP that is based upon an target aircraft, and flies at Mach 0.88, and the S-MART which can carry up to 30 kg of sensors for seven hours; and is a development of the MART, which was used in the Gulf War. The HELIOT is the result of a joint venture with the Italian company DragonFly, and the CRECERELLE made by Dassault Electrónique that includes SWIFT synthetic lens radar for target detection with less

precision at 50 meters. Other designs include the Thomson-CSF VIGILANT, the CL-327 made in conjunction with Canada. The K100 made by CAC that can be used in video-guided attack missions, and the HALE jet-propelled unit that is recaptured from the air by a specially equipped helicopter.

Proposals

From other countries there are several other options, such as the SIVA (Sistema Integrado de Vigilancia Aérea) and the ALO

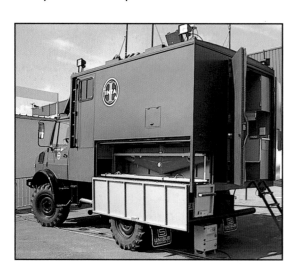

SPANISH
The Instituto Nacional de Técnica Aeroespacial (INTA) of Spain has developed the ALO light observation aircraft that can be folded up for transport in a 3-ton jeep.

(Avión Ligero de Observación) developed by the Spanish Institute of Aerospace Technology. The German LUNA that is designed to provide armored troops with a means of identifying enemy vehicles within a range of 6 miles and the BREVEL derived TAIFUN, that is designed as an attack weapon for destroying high value targets such as control stations. The Greek Sigma NEARCHOS was designed for surveying at medium range and acquiring targets. The Czech SOJKA II/II is produced in collaboration with Hungary. The Dutch SPERWER is produced in collaboration with France.

TRANSPORT

The FOX AT1 can include two supports on each wing for transporting small containers that emit smoke signals to mark a determined position, which help a later attack.

MULTINATIONAL

Adopted by the French, Swedish and Dutch armies, the French Sagem CRECERELLE is the basis of a family of designs at the forefront of the European market.

The British GEC-Marconi PHEONIX and the Aerobotics SPRITE have a superior double rotor. The Italian jet-propelled Meteor MIRACH 26 and 150, together with many other examples which serve the requirments of diverse military forces whether they are for land support, naval survei- llance or for checking the results of air-to-surface raids.

Future

The increasing possibilities and the updating of machines for carrying out more complex tasks, have caused better

engines to be developed to increase operational ranges. The adaptation of advanced sensors associated with real time data transmission systems, for use in any weather conditions, with the aim to destroy the enemy before it can even begin its military movements.

Much more capable and efficient apparatus will come into service to work with more advanced control systems. These will be used for such varied tasks as forest surveillance, the control of illegal waste disposal, the control of crime in urban city centers, traffic control or, among several

FOX
The small FOX AT1, produced by CAC Systems, is transported by a truck that also launches and controls the vehicle.

MULTI-PURPOSE
The Aeroespaciale C22 is a target aircraft that has been designed for use in surveillance, recording images and signals that can be used when the vehicle is recovered.

others, the locating and attacking of central points of the enemy's offence/defence systems.

Designed as a sea born tactical electronic interference system for use by the US Marines, the "Prowler" has constantly been updated to respond to new threats and to be adapted to more advanced configurations. The improvement process, which has been validated by its use in several combat actions, has led to it being chosen by the US Marines and Air Force as a substitute for the electronic warfare aircraft called Grumman EF-111A.

The EA-6B, although essentially designed for EW, has proved such a capable air-

INTERFERER

The basic mission of the "Prowler" is to interfere with enemy communication or radar transmissions, so as to disrupt their activity, although its HARM missiles give it the important secondary function of attacking radar sites or communication centers.

LONG DEVELOPMENT

The current "Prowler" is very different to its predecessors, including many extensions, antennas and protuberances that house the equipment that has been added to it.

plane that the US Air Force has even been known to fit it with missiles and use it on several defence missions.

Interference

The need for an advanced airplane designed to interfere with enemy electronic systems, which could replace the Douglas EA-3B and EKA-3B, derived from the "Skywarrior" bomber, led the US Navy to sign a contract in October 1966 for such a program with Northrop Grumman. Starting from the airframes of the attack aircraft A-6A "Intruder", which had proven ideal for low-flying attack missions, the configuration of the "Prowler" began with the fuselage length being increased by 137 centimeters over that of the A-6; the first flight took place on 25th May 1968, the first presentations in January 1971 and the first operation in the summer of 1972, when they were deployed in South East Asia on the aircraft carrier USS "America".

Production

During its twenty years in production, 170 units of differing configurations have been manufactured, including five prototypes used in tests at the Aircraft Trial Center at Patuxent River in Maryland. The first consisted of 23 units that were complemented, from January 1973 onwards, by another 25 Expanded Capacity (EXCAP) models with better computing systems and the possibility of countering threats on eight frequency lengths.

A more powerful engine and increased interference capabilities were the innovations of the ICAP-1 (Improved Capability Variant) that was ready at the end of 1977, this included the adaptation to this configuration of the units left over from

INTERFERERS

Hanging under the space-saving foldable wings of the "Prowler", we can observe here some of the five containers that hold the powerful ALQ-99F electronic interference system.

CAPABLE

The possibilities of the EA-6B are such that, apart from the US Marines who have been using this plane on their aircraft carriers since the early 1970s, the Air Force has also decided to use this plane on defence missions instead of the EF-111 "Raven".

the earlier variants. The improvement program ended in the early 1980s. At this time Squadron VMAQ-2 was established in the Marine Corps it had received the first of a total of 15 units from October 1978.

In January 1984, the IAP-2 went into service, the prototype of which had been studied since 24th June 1980. Of this variant a total of 72 units were produced at the Calverton factory, different from earlier versions for the inclusion of an AN/AYK-14 processor with more processing power and a larger memory that operated on nine waves, and which was acqui-

red by 12 different squadrons in the mid 1980s.

Improvements

Using the previous model as a base, Block 82 and Block 86 variants have been designed, the numbers referring to the fiscal years in which the programs started. The first presentations took place during January 1986 and July 1988. 23 units were made of the first design and 37 of the second, all capable of firing HARM anti-radar missiles. The latter also have improved communication and signal processing systems that widen the aircraft's flexibility even further.

After analyzing the Advanced Capability, it was decided that, after updating some airplanes as prototypes for trials, the program should be cancelled in 1994, and substituted with the updating of earlier variants such as Block 89A. An experimental version has recently made its first flight from Northrop's plant in St Augustine Florida, characterised by such improvements as new radios, an inertial navigation system that receives data from different satellites via a GPS module, an automatic landing system, new flight instruments and better hardware and software for the AN/AYK-14 mission computer.

Once evaluated and validated, this plane

FUSELAGE

Round, and with the engines cased into its side, the lower fuselage includes the antennas, the interference flares and the components of the undercarriage.

COCKPIT

Configured for two crewmembers and two systems operators, the cockpit, which includes a fixed air refueling tube, is specially designed for work involving electronic interference.

will enter service with the aim of standardizing the fleet to one common model. It is expected that it will stay in service until 2010 or beyond. This model is expected to be adopted by the US Air Force for training crews at Whidbey Island Base in Washington State.

Technical Characteristics

The EA-6B "Prowler" measures 18.24 meters, and is nearly five meters high. When empty it weighs less than 15,000 kilograms, but this weight almost doubles when it carries its maximum load. This airplane, costing 55.7 American dollars to produce, has changed considerably over the years to include all kinds of new equipment in accordance with the demands of modern day combat, including air refueling.

Features

It serves a very specific purpose and the efficiency of the equipment that it carries was quite clear in its successful performance in the Gulf War. For this reason, it has continued to be used on important missions in support of other naval wings and the US Air Force.

Structure

Based on the structural design of the "Intruder", the EA-6B has a distinctively compact fuselage with a double cockpit for

the four crewmembers. Low in the fuselage are small air intakes and the undercarriage is particularly robust.

The radar is protected by a dome over the nose, whil the different antennas that cover different angles and receptive elements are contained within the tail. The wings are slightly arrow shaped with rounded edges, with horizontal one-piece stabilisers and air brakes built into the upper and lower part of their tips.

Activity

Designed for a particular task, it includes APQ-92 navigation and exploration radar in a frontal dome, nearby there is a fixed air refuelling probe. Behind this, the cockpit provides seating for the crew in Martin Baker GRUEA 7 ejector seats, two crew members sit side-by-side, and a further two, also side-by-side sit behind them.

The pilot sits in the left front seat where the controls of the plane are located. At his side sits the ECMO 1 (ECM Officer) who is in charge of navigation, electronic

counter-methods and the launching of self-defence flares. Behind them sit ECMO 2 and 3 who study the display screens, on which appear data concerning any located threats, to which the appropriate interference is applied. They use a PRB Associates AN/TSQ-142 tactical support system and a Teledyne Systems AN/ASN-123 navigation kit.

Equipment

A very powerfully updated AN/AYK-14 computer processes the signals recorded from long distance by the antennas built into the tail rudder and the container above, and presents the collected information to the ECMOs. After analyzing the enemy's radar signals and transmissions, the ALQ-99F system, carried in five under-wing containers, activates by transmitting high power signals that nullify those of the enemy systems. Each of these containers includes an exciter, two powerful transmitters and, in the front part, a four-rotor wind-powered Garret generator. This works on dynamic pressure and produces the 27 kilowatts necessary for its independent functioning as long as the plane is flying at at least 240 mph.

Possibilities

Driven by two small Pratt & Whitney

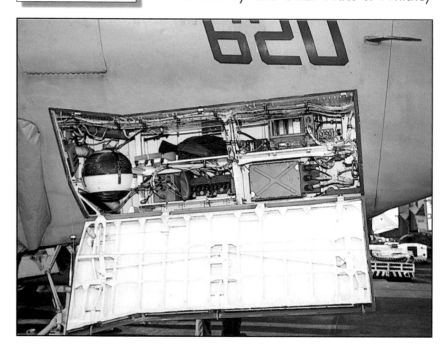

TECHNICAL CHARACTERISTICS EA-6B "PROWLER"

COST:	55.7 million dollars		PROPULSION:	
DIMENSIONS:			Two Pratt & Whitney J52-P-408A jet engines providing thrust of 5,080 kilograms	
Length	18,24 m			
Height	4,95 m		**FEATURES:**	
Wingspan	16,15 m		Maximum altitude	12,550 m
Wing surface	29,13 m²		Maximum speed	629 mph
WEIGHT:			Speed with containers	589 mph
Empty	14.321 kg		Take-off distance	814 m
Maximum	29.483 kg		Landing distance	579 m
Internal fuel	8.712 l		Maximum distance	2,317 miles
External fuel	5.710 l		Operating range	1,061 miles

J52-P-408A turbojet engines that offer a total of 10,160 kilograms of thrust, this airplane can operate at speeds up to 628 mph. It can up its range to some 1,800 miles when it substitutes two of its underwing containers with auxiliary fuel tanks.

It can be used for different kinds of activity because each of the five containers is dedicated to the neutralization of different frequency waves at the same time, depen-

SHIPS

Each of the US Marine Wings assigned to aircraft carriers include four EA-6B electronic aircraft airplanes, three of which can be seen here on board U.S.S. "Kennedy"

ding on the kind of threat the mission is confronted by. If necessary, some of these can be replaced by Texas Instruments AGM-88A HARM anti-radar missiles that can destroy sites possessing such radar. This missile guides itself towards the source of the signal it is receiving, giving off an explosive charge on impact that should cause the destruction of the transmission or detection system.

The elimination of submarines and ships requires a series of armaments designed to comply with the perimeters of specific tasks. Whil submarines can be destroyed by homing torpedoes, mines, and depth charges. The ships on the surface are attacked with guided missiles so as to avoid the powerful air defences that such vessels can deploy by attacking from beyond the horizon.

Threat

The eternal struggle to control the seas changed tactics, firstly with the introduction of ground-based aircraft, and later of ship born aircraft. Self-defence techniques and different procedures had to be adopted.

MULTI-ROLE

Derived from the anti-surface "Harpoon" and made by McDonnell Douglas, the SLAM (Standoff and Land Attack Missile) is being made for the US Marines and includes an updated warhead for destroying land targets, as it recently displayed in an attack on an Iraqi hydroelectric plant.

LIGHT

Used during the Falklands Conflict and the Gulf War, the anti-surface missile "Sea Skua" has been designed to provide naval helicopters with a means of attacking and destroying objects on the surface. Only one is needed to destroy a patrol boat, but several more are necessary to eliminate a frigate.

Submarines

Since the advent of the nuclear submarine, they are considerably harder to detect. Before, the battery recharging process meant they had to travel near the surface and raise a mast to the surface to receive the oxygen which was needed to fuel the diesel engine. Moreover, newer submarines rely upon ever more modern equipment, that serves to further disguise their presence.

The airplanes and helicopters whose task it is to destroy them, identified by the prefix anti-submarine, do not have an easy task in detecting them. They use a large collection of different tools to find out the exact position of their enemies such as radar, sonar buoys, magnetic abnormality detectors and smoke sensors. Once located, they can be attacked by the same aircraft or the data obtained can be passed on to more powerful aircraft that are better equipped to totally destroy the vessel.

Destruction

If the decision is made to destroy the submarine, different weapons will be used depending on where it is. If it is near the surface, something that is only likely if the submarine has been damaged, unguided rocket launchers or heavy machine guns will cause sufficient damage to its structure.

It is more probable that the submarine

will be submerged at a depth that would depend on the specific craft. A conventional submarine can rarely go deeper than 300 meters, but a nuclear submarine can reach depths of 900. Depth charges, such as the British Mk11 or the Swedish SAM 204 are containers that include a large quantity of explosives and a system that makes them explode at a given depth. This rather limits their use, and they are often backed up by modern mines, such as the American "Quickstrike", the Russian AMD or the MRP-80, that have the ability to only explode on detection of the exact signals that are produced by a certain naval unit.

ANTI-SUBMARINE

Light torpedoes can be fired from helicopters or maritime patrol airplanes like this French "Atlantique". Its mission is to locate, pursue and strike the shell of submarines that will be destroyed on impact with the huge explosive head.

IN PRODUCTION

The US Marines' order for seven hundred AGM-84H SLAM-ER was started in March 1997 and should be completed by 2004.

The mines are usually placed where they are most likely to catch the enemy, such as the approaches to naval bases or obligatory passages.

Some, but very few, countries also have nuclear tactical mines that are left in the zones in which it is believed that the submarines are moving. The enormous force of the explosion that these mines give off is sufficient to break the resistant shell of the submarine's structure.

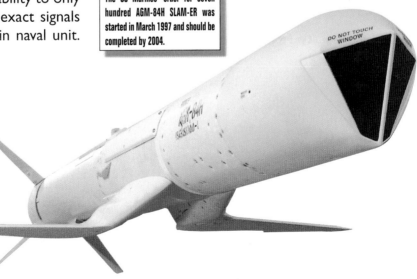

Torpedoes

However, the most normal solution is the homing torpedo, a powerful, compact and reliable weapon for use in a wide range of operations. Placed on the under-wing supports of helicopters or in the holds of airplanes, light western torpedoes tend to have diameters of 324 millimeters, although the Swedes make 400 mm variants, while the Russians do not have a standard measurement.

Widely distributed throughout the world is the American Honeywell Mk46, of which the 5 NEARTIP model is the most celebrated. Its features include a weight of 230 kilograms, an active and passive homing device, a speed of 42 mph and a maximum range of 6.6 miles. The Mk50 "Barracuda", faster and with a longer range thanks to its short circuit chemical engine, was introduced as a replacement. It has a homing device that is specially designed to hunt Russian third-generation submarines of "Akula" and "Sierra" class.

The Swedes, who have had several encounters with Russian submarines entering their waters to spy on their fleet's activity, use class 42 and 43 torpedoes that are known for their explosive heads of 45 or 50 kg, and have a range of 12 miles their speed can be programmed in relation to that of their target. Other models include the Italian Whitehead A-244/S, in service since 1987 and its substitute the A-290, the

> **HUNTER**
>
> Naval helicopters take on missions in which they have to attack surface vessels and submarines. One example is the Eurocopter AS 565 SB "Panther" armed with light AS 15 TT missiles, which are powerful enough to destroy small vessels such as patrol boats, tugs and minesweepers.

> **STEALTH**
>
> Using the latest Stealth technology, the Norwegian firm Kongsberg has designed the New anti-Ship Missile that weighs 420 kilograms and has an operational range of over 60 miles thanks to its turbojet engine and passive infrared homing device.

British GEC Marconi "Sting Ray", which has some outstanding features, the French "Mùrene" and the Russian APR-2E, which reaches 69 mph and S-3V, whose diameter is only 212 mm.

Anti-surface missions

Surface vessels expect to be attacked in a varity of ways, this is why they carry so many defence systems. These can vary from light portable missile systems to highly advanced multiple launchers, light machine guns to last second point defence systems.

Different systems are needed to cope

with these, from the aforementioned torpedoes to different types of bomb or decoy chaff, the latter used for causing damage to unescorted and unprotected ships such as amphibious vessels, tankers, freighters and tugs. However, even these often have simple weapon defence systems that can cause problems for such attacks.

Autonomous long or short-range guided missiles that can hit a target despite being fired from a distance are used to avoid the possibility of the aircraft being struck down.

Helicopter missiles

Missiles are usually fired from naval helicopters which are transported on anti-submarine and general escort frigates. They usually weigh less than 200 kg so that they can be attached to the aircraft transporting them, they are propelled by a small motor towards targets to within an 18 mile range and include a warhead that can cause collateral damage to electronic systems and weapons, or sink lighter vessels. It may take more than one of them to eliminate a frigate or a destroyer.

Amongst the models in service are the Aeroespaciale AS 15TT, which the French marines use on "Lynx" and "Dauphin" heli-

ROCKETS
P-3C "Orion" airplanes of Patrol Squadron VP-45, stationed at Jacksonville Naval Station, Florida, fire "Zoonie" rockets at a surface target on the Puerto Rican coast.

copters, the British Aerospace "Sea Skua", used against Argentinean ships in the Falklands Conflict and against Iraqi patrols in the Gulf. The Norwegian Kongsberg "Penguin", also used by American SH-60s, the Italian "Marte" and the Hughes "Maverik". It is also possible to use some land missiles for the task too, such as the "Hellfire".

Heavy

The notorious success of Argentinean pilots with Aeroespaciale AM-39 "Exocet" missiles, which caused considerable damage to the British destroyer "Sheffield" and the container ship "Atlantic Conveyor" in the Falklands Conflict, or the action in which the Iraqi Mirage F-1 pilots attacked and almost sank the American frigate "Stark" FFG-31 with the same French product, have proven the destructive power of this weapon. It can be transported to the attack zone on the appropriate attack airplane, fighter-bomber, maritime patrol aircraft or, possibly, from helicopters such as

ANTI-SUBMARINE
British light helicopters use "Sting Ray" torpedoes and Mk11 model 3 depth charges to take out submarines under the water.

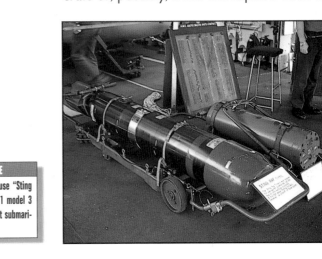

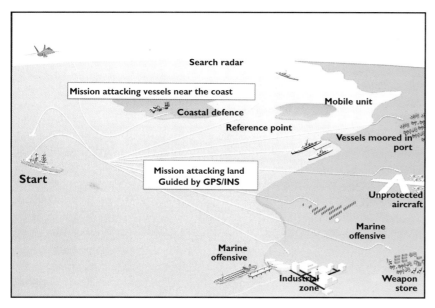

Search radar

Mission attacking vessels near the coast

Mobile unit

Coastal defence

Reference point

Vessels moored in port

Mission attacking land Guided by GPS/INS

Start

Unprotected aircraft

Marine offensive

Marine offensive

Industrial zone

Weapon store

the French "Super Frelón" or the multinational "Merlin".

With an operational radius of about 60 miles, the destructive capacity to take a naval unit of 4,000 tons out of combat. The ability to fly just above the surface of the water to avoid detection and to make evasive moves to dodge attacks that could prevent it reaching its target, this kind of missile weighs around 600 kg and needs powerful aircraft to transport it. Among the more common examples are the German DASA-LFK "Kormoran", the Matra

Bae Dynamics "Sea Eagle", which is undergoing a Life Extension Program, the Swedish Saab-Bofors RBS 15F, the Russian X-31 and X-35, and the ubiquitous AGM-84 "Harpoon" of which the more celebrated variants are Block II and SLAM.

New missiles will enter service in the future with stealth technology for avoiding radar, such as the American SLAM-ER and the Norwegian NSM, and the current supersonic designs, which travel so fast that it is hard for the enemy to react in time, will be updated. These include the Chinese FL-7, the Russian "Raduga" and X-15C, the Israeli "Gabriel" IV and a new American model derived from the Boeing "Fasthawk" that will fly at between Mach 6 and 8.

The "Harpoon" missile

The anti-surface missile "Harpoon" is an American design that is widely distributed throughout the world. It can be fired from aerial, naval or coastal positions for the attack of both still and moving targets.

ITALIAN
The Marte MK2A is a light anti-surface missile made by the Italian firm Oto Melara and is well known for its use on helicopters, light training jets and fighter-bombers